STARTUP

AN INSIDER'S GUIDE TO LAUNCHING AND RUNNING A BUSINESS

KEVIN READY

Apress®

Startup: An Insider's Guide to Launching and Running a Business

ISBN-13 (pbk): 978-1-4302-4218-5

ISBN-13 (electronic): 978-1-4302-4220-8

President and Publisher: Paul Manning
Lead Editor: Jeff Olson
Editorial Board: Steve Anglin, Mark Beckner, Ewan Buckingham, Gary Cornell, Morgan Ertel, Jonathan Gennick, Jonathan Hassell, Robert Hutchinson, Michelle Lowman, James Markham, Matthew Moodie, Jeff Olson, Jeffrey Pepper, Douglas Pundick, Ben Renow-Clarke, Dominic Shakeshaft, Gwenan Spearing, Matt Wade, Tom Welsh
Editorial Assistant: Rita Fernando
Copy Editor: Damon Larson
Compositor: Apress Production
Indexer: BIM Indexing & Proofreading Services
Cover Designer: Anna Ishchenko

Distributed to the book trade worldwide by Springer Science+Business Media New York, 233 Spring Street, 6th Floor, New York, NY 10013. Phone 1-800-SPRINGER, fax (201) 348-4505, e-mail orders-ny@springer-sbm.com, or visit www.springeronline.com.

For information on translations, please e-mail rights@apress.com, or visit www.apress.com.

Apress and friends of ED books may be purchased in bulk for academic, corporate, or promotional use. eBook versions and licenses are also available for most titles. For more information, reference our Special Bulk Sales–eBook Licensing web page at www.apress.com/bulk-sales.

TO KAZUKO, CONNOR, MITCHEL, MAE, AND RAYMOND

Contents

About the Author

Kevin Ready loves building things and helping people to build things. Over the last 20 years, he has built, run, consulted for, and advised numerous startups and businesses. For him, there is nothing more interesting than understanding business models and the problems that entrepreneurs come up against in their markets. As he says often, "It is my work and my play. I never get tired of it."

Born into a engineering family, Ready started his first company right out of college. While the venture was a success, he saw the limitations to scaling the business. As the Internet era took shape, he joined the "tech wave" through the late 1990s, starting several online businesses. Years before Facebook, he was a founder of a social networking site with nearly one million users. Later, he and a partner spun off and sold a digital mapping business, then moved on to become an online software and media retail business that merged with a larger rival in 2008. That same year, he became a partner at an online real estate business that was in crisis mode. By applying the lessons presented in this book, he helped turn the business around. Just 13 months later, it was acquired by a company in the newspaper industry. That business—where he still works as technical director and strategist—now brings in millions of dollars of profit per year and touches over 4 million consumers monthly.

In addition to his entrepreneurial ventures, he has worked in engineering positions at Dell Computer and Toshiba, and as an executive at Classified Ventures, LLC.

Acknowledgments

Many thanks to those people that have inspired my work as an entrepreneur, and to those who freely gave of their time and knowledge to assist me in putting this book together.

I especially appreciate the time I spent with my friend Joseph Wright, his father Wayne Wright, Sr., and their family during my teenage years. Observing this wonderfully entrepreneurial family, I decided that business building was a lifestyle choice worth emulating.

Special thanks to Dr. Fernando Macias, Dr. Ken Price, George Mora, and Daniel Castro, for their substantial investments of time to assist me with this manuscript.

Also great thanks to Jeff Olson, my editor from Apress. Your persistence and patience are the difference that made the difference.

Preface

What we *do* is a function of what we know, and what we have experienced and come to understand. As entrepreneurs, we encounter myriad difficult, novel, and challenging situations that *normal* people will never be faced with, and we build up a library of such experiences over time. In the entrepreneurial world, this is sometimes aptly described as *scar tissue*, and it is with some level of respect and admiration that we say that somebody has a lot of it. Some of these experiences and lessons stand out above the others and grow to serve as a basis for the entrepreneur's decision-making ever after. This book is about scar tissue, about lessons learned, and about how we can use those lessons to make business less painful, less difficult, and more profitable.

A great interest of mine is helping motivated people to start their own businesses. I especially enjoy working with people who are absolutely *excellent* at something. These are folks that have an area of excellence that they have developed over many years. They have realized that they could provide greater value for themselves and their families if they focus all of their time and energy on exercising that area of excellence as a business, in the form of a startup. This is a great leap, and it is one of the most exciting moves you can make. What most people find, however, is that their area of excellence alone is not enough to carry them through the challenge of wrapping a business around it. Their core skill set (programming, DNA analysis, etc.) needs to be mated with new business skills to make it all work.

As an example, my friend John (who is a highly skilled PhD microbiologist) recently started his own genetics company. He knows DNA sequencing up and down; he has been doing it for years. It was easy for him to imagine leaving the university research environment and applying his skills for his own customers. It was so easy to imagine, in fact, that John actually quit his university research job, took out a business loan, bought a lab full of equipment, and is now on his own—and is realizing at a visceral level that he *must* quickly become excellent at a long list of entrepreneurial skills that he has never thought about before. As of the writing of this preface, he has all of the trappings of a business, except he has no customers yet! This book is for John, and any other people with a robust competency and excellence in their specialties who want to make a business out of it.

I have spent a lot of time helping people like John. In consulting with them, my primary objective is to help them reframe their understanding in some very particular ways. A *reframe* is a change in the aggregate understanding we have of a situation or process—a change in the perspective we have on it. An expert and a novice can look at the same situation and come to very different conclusions about what it means. This is true for everything that we do in life. In business, there are a few fundamental, overarching, and important reframes that, once understood, empower you to perform at a higher level—with more efficiency and a greater capability for your business to survive. This book is, at its core, a compendium of critical reframes for the entrepreneur.

So How Did I Become an Entrepreneur?

After years of education, every college graduate is faced with the same question: "What do I want to do?" When I was a nearing the end of college, I knew that I wanted to be an entrepreneur. I had grown up in an engineering family. I studied engineering in school and I wanted to build a tech business, but I did not want to go to business school to learn how. My decision was to do a "real-world" MBA program of my own construction—a starter business. I would find a business that had a low barrier to entry (since I did not have any money) and would leverage whatever skills I had. I wanted to construct a real-life laboratory that would expose me to the ins and outs of the full-time, man-in-charge entrepreneurial experience. I called this plan that I was setting up for myself "Mailroom to the Board Room." I wanted to start at the lowest and most basic form of work possible, and build for myself a set of experiences in which I could learn the lessons needed to grow from the simplest kind of business to running multi-million-dollar corporations.

I started with a $5,000 loan and a simple desire to start my own business. Two decades later, I have been through three successful corporate transactions—the latest of which is now reaching nearly 5 million customers per month.

Along the way I did the following:

- Opened a construction business, learning how to run a startup the hard way: by doing it.

- Moved on to building an Internet services company, and building our own data center from scratch.

- Launched a social networking business with nearly 1 million users, years before Facebook.

- Created a digital mapping data company, earned a portfolio of *Fortune* 500 customers, and sold the business to private equity investors.

- Was a partner in an online retail business, eventually merging with a larger competitor.

- Joined a 50-person startup company—with the challenging objective to turn it around and get it acquired. In just one year we had rebuilt the brand and earned an acquisition by a larger competitor. We had phenomenal growth, and soon became the fourth-largest apartment real estate web site in the United States.

- Consulted for and helped entrepreneurs with startups in countries all over the world.

This book shares some of what I have learned along the way.

How to Read This Book

This book is organized into chapters that cover the most important building blocks of any startup: Setting the Stage, Core Lessons, Marketing, Building a Team, Communication Matters, Strategic Thinking, and Exiting Your Business.

The chapters themselves are composed of individual, discrete lessons that stand alone and can be read independent of the other parts of the chapter. Several of my favorite books follow this standalone format, and I have followed that paradigm here. The compact size of each section is deliberate in that each is a distillation of one or two standalone concepts from my entrepreneurial experience. I believe that your ability to understand and remember these ideas is best supported by getting to the point quickly, and keeping the volume of text to a minimum.

Each subsection has a title that is intended to support your recall of the subject—a mnemonic key to assist your memory. In my businesses and my consulting with entrepreneurs, these are phrases or keywords that I frequently teach and use as labels for the important ideas within.

If you're a new or aspiring entrepreneur, I recommend reading the book from the beginning, and working your way through the chapters in order. If you're an experienced entrepreneur, this book can be read straight through or by sections in random order without loss of congruence.

Come Fly with Me

I was recently fortunate enough to be slicing a brilliant blue summer sky over Napa Valley at the controls of a sleek two-person glider. The flight instructor in the back seat gave me a great piece of advice when I asked how to gain altitude. She said, "Look for the biggest birds, and follow them." You see, large birds gain altitude by riding thermals (not flapping). For them, the air up there is their natural environment, and they know how to make the most of it. As a (mostly) land-bound mammal, I didn't have much idea of how to get what I wanted in that aerial environment. Thermals are completely invisible—and startling when you come upon them, because they whack you like a tornado looking for a double-wide. Spotting an upwardly spiraling hawk and following its lead with a similar flight pattern was a great strategy to begin to understand the mostly invisible, rapidly changing, and complex environment I was in.

This is a great strategy for aspiring entrepreneurs as well: find people riding the currents in the way you'd like to and then do what they do. Better yet, sit down with that bird and share a bottle of bourbon—get him to open up and fill you in on some of his flying secrets. That in a way describes this book: it is an intimate conversation, where anything goes, with the end goal of helping you to understand the invisible inside experience of being an entrepreneur. If you want to learn how to identify opportunities, fluently interact with markets, and grow a business of your own, then this book can help.

Let's do some flying together.

Kevin Ready
http://kevinready.com
December 2011

Setting the Stage

As we get started on this business adventure together, I want to share with you what I mean when I use the word *entrepreneur*. The following definition sums it up succinctly:

> *An entrepreneur is a risk-taker who invests his time, energy, and/or capital to create a new product, process, or service that has resonance within a given community.*

Let's look at the implications of this idea.

Entrepreneurship and Resonance

Let's flesh this out a bit. An entrepreneur needs to find a way to interact with people (preferably lots of people) in a way that *resonates* with them. This means that the product or service attracts their participation and buy-in. In physics, resonance occurs when a pattern in one system causes surrounding systems to begin to vibrate or move in a similar pattern. This is exactly what entrepreneurs do. This can be social entrepreneurship—for example, President Jimmy Carter working with Habitat for Humanity (lots of resonance and buy-in there). However, it is usually business oriented, such as Jeff Bezos' Amazon.com. His creation certainly resonates with people, and they demonstrate this with their purchasing power. They keep going back to Amazon again and again.

Another great example of buy-in and resonance can be seen in San Francisco with Blue Bottle Coffee Company. It is an immensely popular coffee business, in an already crowded market. Even with Starbucks and numerous other options available in the marketplace, the 30-minute line of devoted coffee drinkers queued up every morning stands as a literal testament to the resonance the company created. Where did this resonance come from? A high-quality product, delivered in a way that people want. *"It's really about an appreciation for unnecessary beauty,"* founder James Freeman says, *"and a willingness to work for it."* [1]

Note   An entrepreneur is a builder of resonance.

In order to develop resonance, a startup has to start with a product or service. Selecting that starting point requires a few perspectives that are vital and definitely worth recognizing. Let's look at each in turn.

Entrepreneurs Create Something New

Entrepreneurship always starts with a proposition: you are going to solve someone's problem—specifically:

- You have information or insight that other people don't have.

- You have a unique product.

- You will deliver an existing product to a group that does not have it.

- You will deliver an existing product in a new way, which could be faster, cheaper, or better.

---

[1] *Fortune* magazine, September 26, 2011

It Is Compelling

The business idea is important enough that, when properly executed, it will trigger a specific customer group to reach into their pockets, pull out their money, and pay you for it.

You Can Scale It

Does your idea structurally have enough potential transactions to make enough money? If you buckle down tight and build this business, identify how big it can get, and what resources you will need to get there.

If you are marketing your own time as a consultant, for instance, is it scalable to your needs? You only have 24 hours a day to sell—and will occasionally need to sleep and eat. So your inventory of product is limited.

If you are selling products, what are the physical limitations on how much product you can get your hands on and connect with customers? These include the following:

- *Product availability*: If you are selling large, complex products, how many can you actually manufacture per year?

- *Demand*: What will the market bear in terms of transactions that you can compete for?

Play it out, and see what the outer bounds of your idea look like in terms of scale, product availability, and demand of the market.

You Can Control It

Having chosen a product or service, can you control the vital elements of the business? These include things like access to merchandise, licensing, and so forth. This is a structural aspect of the business that you are responsible for figuring out before you jump in.

- What political, legislative, or economic factors are you depending on to stay in business? For example, building a vehicle emissions testing device as a core product is highly dependent on having states legislate that such testing is required.

- If your chosen business model is dependent on a third-party license or company, what are the risks associated with that dependency? What guarantees do you have for the long-term stability and availability of that relationship? For example, becoming an independent agent of an insurance company creates a clear dependence on that company's strength and evolving reputation.

- An example of this is the current fad of serve-yourself yogurt shops, which is hitting hard in Austin, Texas. A dozen such shops have opened there in the last 18 months. These market players cannot control how many more of these will pop up and eat up local market share from them—they just have to watch what happens.

- An example of "control done right" is a car dealership. When you are lucky enough to get the go-ahead to open a Honda or Lexus dealership, you are given a region wherein only you will represent the brand. That is a powerful type of control.

- If you are licensing a solar technology from China to build a customer base in Europe, can you negotiate an exclusive right to do so? Or will any company with an interest in the technology be able to do the same thing?

- If you have a novel technology of some kind, can you get patents to cover your invention and make it defensible?

Exercise: Get a whiteboard and visually draw out the relationships between your idea, the customers, the dependencies (licenses, product, sales channels), your staff, and any other details you can think of. Become fluent in the story and explore the relationships thoroughly before committing to any particular strategy or business model.

A Ticket to the Game

Most folks think that building a product or packaging a great service is the hardest part of becoming a successful business owner. The thought is something along the lines of, "If we can just build the web site, or open the restaurant, or create the widget—then we are going to start making money!"

Building it, opening it, or inventing it is often the easy part. The hard part is usually what comes next—connecting with customers, communicating your value, and convincing them to pull out their wallets to give you money.

Figuring out exactly how you will *connect the product* with enough customers in a short enough time span so that you survive, and grow to thrive—that's where the real work awaits.

To be successful in business you do have to have a great product; a product that is developed and ready to go. This alone takes a great deal of time, effort, and investment. However, this great achievement is nothing more than *a ticket to the game*. It is the cost of admission that allows you to enter the coliseum and fight the battle for the attention of your customers. And this is competition against those who are already in the market trying to make a dollar in your chosen space. This process of connecting your idea with customers is your business. Not only that, you have to connect your idea given a rigid set of constraints:

- *Time*: How long can you go before you establish a base level of product sales?

- *Money*: How much money you have for marketing determines what strategies are available to you. Never use your whole budget for product development—make sure to allocate a significant amount of money for the marketing effort.

- *Product Category Awareness:* Is there already awareness in the market for what your category of product does?

- *Brand Awareness:* Do you have any market awareness associated with your particular product or service that you can leverage? Are you starting from scratch?

- *Competitive Messaging*: How much messaging is already being directed at your customers by competitors?

- *Non-competitive Messaging*: How heavily is your customer base being messaged by other businesses that are not related to what you are offering? (You are in competition with them, too, when you are trying to get a customer's attention.)

Takeaways: Building a product is nothing more than a step in your business. For most companies, the hard part—*the business part*—is the process of connecting that product or service with customers given a limited set of resources.

Nobody Cares About Your Business

When consulting with entrepreneurs that are struggling to get a business off the ground, I often end up telling them this:

> I read a great book on starting your own business. It's the most important book on the subject you could ever read—and it only had two words in it.
> Those two words were "nobody cares."

To close the story and make the point, I tell them that as an entrepreneur, your *entire job* is to make those two tiny, awful words wrong.

That's it. Make people care about what you are doing.

The fact of the matter is that at first, people won't care. People are busy. People won't know who you are when you start out, and they won't go out of their way to find out. As you create a business, and move beyond your product to the point where you are figuring out how to connect your product with the market, you realize that the whole purpose behind your effort is to get people to care about what you do. If you are in the computer business, it is not just about computers. If you are in the pizza business, it is not just about pizza. The best product in the world is just a starting point, and it won't make you a dollar unless you can figure out how to make that product relevant to the lives of your customers and get them to understand that relevance. Having a great product helps, but that alone is not enough.

This bias toward customer indifference is a reality of the market. But to tell you the truth, I like the fact that getting into markets is tough, because that means that it is *tough for my competitors too*, and will serve to keep the folks in your market that aren't smart enough or fast enough from hogging the swing set for too long.

What Is a Business?

Too often, business owners, managers, and decision-makers get fooled by the way they use language into thinking that their business is a "thing." It is not. It is convenient and even necessary to use a noun to refer to your business when communicating with people, but when you visualize it for yourself, make sure you *don't ever* do so. One of the lessons I have brought along to all of the companies that I have worked at and consulted for is the following:

> *Your business is not a noun. It is a verb. It is a "happening" and a "doing." It is nothing less than the sum total of the actions and thoughts of every employee and customer. It is the result-in-motion of all of the things that the people who participate in your business do each and every day.*

Mentally framing your business in this way is an easy and useful step toward understanding it and how its complexity is organized between ideas, your staff, your customers, and the wider market. If you are visualizing the business as a noun (an object of some kind), your model of understanding is inherently missing much of its complexity. By promoting your visualization from a noun (static) to a verb, you automatically give yourself a much more complex modeling paradigm. You will immediately get closer to the reality of dance-like complexity found in all businesses as they grow and operate.

The Boat

Most people are employees working for other people. This employment may chafe them a bit from time to time, but they are sacrificing a bit of freedom for the stability. They usually aspire to become leaders in their environment, in part to grow their salary, and in part to ease the chafing—and to have more control over their own lives. Inherent in this is the idea that you "plug in" to a structure that other people have created (a corporation, university, etc.). The idea of advanced education (getting an MBA for example), is a way to open options for plugging in to the structure in some advantageous manner. This is the most common work pattern in the developed world—finding a company to work for.

Some make a different choice: to find their own path, and take the burden of owning something from top to bottom and being responsible for the outcome in a way that others will never understand. Here are the characters in a parable that usefully describes what I am talking about.

The Employee

He is riding in a big boat. Cold seas thrash outside, but in the boat's sturdy, rigid interior it feels relatively warm and dry. There are waves and movement that can be felt inside the boat, but he feels safe most of the time. He knows that there is the threat of the boat sinking or being asked to walk the plank if he makes a mistake, but he tries not to worry about that most of the time. He has a set of duties onboard that he attends to. He gets health insurance and a steady paycheck; his life feels safe, except it is not as stimulating as it could be. Looking out of the window at the strange lands outside, he thinks, "I wonder what else is out there? Where is this boat going anyway? The captain knows. Probably."

The Entrepreneur

He has no boat, but has a dream in mind. He heads to the forest. Once there, he *makes* an axe and then proceeds to cut down trees to make a boat. This is tiring, but somehow the work propels him. Next, he has to figure out how to get the boat into the water, how to waterproof it, how to repair it, how to steer it—and he does so. Eventually it is safe enough for employees to ride in it along with him. When the storms come, all eyes turn to him for answers. When treasure is found or blue-sky sailing takes place, it is to his credit. Eventually he hires a captain to steer, and he settles on the best of the beaches found during his voyage. At night he has vivid dreams of forests, waves, and opportunity.

The major difference between the characters in this tale comes down to two words: *ownership mentality*. Being an entrepreneur forces you to address every detail of an operation—to own the details from top to bottom (lest ye be owned by them, and fail). Starting from scratch, and having nobody to fall back on changes you. Your vision widens and deepens, your sense of resourcefulness grows, and your tendency to take action independently without having someone else prompt you becomes second nature.

Because of this, entrepreneurs can make excellent employees. If you can get them on staff and keep them interested, they can create a great deal of value for you. Truly a rare and valuable commodity.

Launch Strategies

There are a number of different strategies for launching a business, and they depend primarily on the amount of resources you have available.

The Soft Launch

What do you do when you have an idea and no cash? Keep your day job, that's what. Being an entrepreneur is not an all-or-nothing proposition. By doing a *soft launch* of your business, you can scout out the territory with low risk by continuing whatever career you have, but starting to put feelers out into the market in support of your idea.

Build a web site, and sell your product or services at a small scale. This allows you to gather information about the viability of your plan, satisfy your itch to build something, and experience a good bit of the adventure without putting yourself or your family in a dangerous financial position.

Never underestimate the value of a steady paycheck and the benefits that come with a good job, such as health insurance. It takes a lot of progress on a startup to get to the point where it can provide comparable security (probably years).

Jumping In

This kind of business launch is what I think most people think of when starting a business: putting all of your chips on the table and playing your hand—win it all or lose it all. This is a risky proposition, and not to be taken lightly. The benefit of doing this is that you can give your full attention to the project, and you can move fast. This is appropriate when the window of opportunity for your business will only be open for a short time. The caveat here is that you cannot jump in without some pool of resources to draw upon, or a very manageable risk profile (such as no family to support). That is how I started—I was single and just out of college. I could afford to take the risks, and jumped in and made it work. It changed me forever.

Another example of the "jumping in" can be seen in a fellow entrepreneur, and good friend. He is so determined to make his business work, he took out a second mortgage on his house to pay for operational expenses—and he has a wife and kids.

Clearly, jumping in is much easier when you have capital reserves to work from, whether from investors or your own bank account.

Joining Someone Else's Party

You may end up with an opportunity to join a business venture that is entrepreneurial, but already funded and in motion. In this scenario, you have the benefits of a paycheck and corporate niceties, but also the open environment of a startup where your entrepreneurial skills can be applied to define a business that is not yet well formed.

The downside of this is that you will have to negotiate for even a piece of equity, as opposed to being the founder and deciding equity distributions for others. You are also likely to be compensated as an employee for the most part.

And depending on the organization, not being the top guy probably means that you won't get much credit for your ideas.

Different Kinds of Work

One of the most important pieces of advice I ever got was from my father. He told me that it was critical to be *paid for your thoughts, and not your labor.* This is quite obvious to me now, but it was revelatory to me at the time. When you think about the options available to you as an employee or business owner, the model you choose has structural features, which provide both opportunity and limitation. Let's use the construction business as a storyboard for taking a look at some fundamentals of work.

The Laborer: Shoveling Dirt

On the construction site, this type of work has the lowest barrier to entry, and is the simplest business model known to man. You work and get paid for it. You are trading your hours for dollars in a linear sense. Work more hours, get more money. When you stop shoveling, you stop getting paid. Here are some observations for you to consider:

- You have little control over your own schedule.

- You have little flexibility in how you do your work.

- Your labor does not scale—if you are not shoveling, you don't get paid.

- When you are shoveling, you don't have time to do anything else.

- It's hard to make your labor unique and thus more valuable. Lots of people can shovel, so the wage will be low. Compensation goes up as what you do (or how you do it) becomes more scarce in the market.

Some examples of laborers include day laborers, and most programmers and creatives (e.g., designers). Many high-status people are in this category as well, including most doctors and lawyers. In fact, most people in our society fit into this description of work.

Like a Boss: Have Other People Shovel Dirt for You

So you are getting smart and you hire a group of guys to shovel dirt for you, leaving you responsible for making the deals. You get paid for the job and you pay your people for being shovelers. This is the start of entrepreneurship, which means

- You have more control over your schedule.

- You have some flexibility over how your team does the work.

- Your business nonetheless scales poorly in many cases—you will often not be able to make a dollar unless you are there on the work site to point and explain to the shovelers what they have to do.

- You have some amount of time to plan.

- It's hard to make this unique—lots of people can field a team of shovelers, and the fundamental work (shoveling) can be obtained easily in the market.

Examples in this category include contract programming companies, cleaning services, creative agencies. These are businesses that usually have a principal founder that selectively hires talented employees to scale his or her ability to deliver a service.

The Big Boss: Hire a Team of Managers to Manage the Shovelers

You are moving up in the world now, which means you have lots of control over your schedule, but you have to make sure your managers are incentivized to protect your interests with your customers.

- At this point, you may be less concerned with how the team does the actual work.

- On the plus side, the business scales up to your capacity to arrange work for your teams.

- You have lots of time to plan.

- The fundamental proposition (shoveling) is still constrained by its easy availability in the marketplace.

An example in this category is any service company that has grown a layer of managers beneath the owner (software, financial services, construction, legal, etc.).

The Impresario: Invent a New Shovel and Sell It to the Shovelers

Now this is starting to get interesting! You can sell tools to the shovelers and then make money from every one of the many people out there who shovel either for a living or at home. This is the *B to C* (business-to-consumer) operations model.

Your two main concerns are

1. Designing a shovel that is different in some fundamental way than those already available. Is it lighter? Perhaps it is cheaper? Has a better handle? Or is it a different, more efficient shape?

2. Getting this shovel into the hands of the laborers.

With this model, you have lots of control over your product and your schedule. Marketing may be difficult, however, because you have to reach lots of individual customers who are spread out across the market.

Steve Jobs and Michael Dell are two examples of people in this type of position. They both created products that were targeted at a population of consumers—resulting in a large volume of relatively low dollar transactions.

The Impresario Grande: Invent a Shovel and Sell It to the Big Bosses

You are now directing your marketing at a smaller group of larger customers, the big bosses. This is the *B to B* (business-to-business) operations model. Marketing is more targeted when you have to reach only a few large customers instead of a wide population of small customers. This business model carries different opportunities and demands than the B to C business model, and although it is the last example in a progression of business types, it is not necessarily superior to the others—just different.

- Each transaction may be more difficult to get, but it is probably worth much more money and will likely result in multiple transactions over time.

- Successful B to B organizations have the capital, relationships, marketing, and manufacturing expertise to get into other areas. Moving beyond shovels, how about screwdrivers, saws, and specialty tools?

- Fewer customers means a less diversified customer base—which can be a risk.

- Major pivots are sometimes necessary for B to B businesses. An example of this is IBM, which pivoted from being a hardware vendor to being a services provider, because after decades of selling businesses computer hardware, the market evolved to where this was no longer profitable. On the other hand, companies like Procter & Gamble (B to C) have a diverse audience, and many products and will not likely ever have to pivot into a different business focus—there will always be a market for shampoo!

Larry Ellison of Oracle and Marc Benioff of Salesforce.com are two examples of this type of entrepreneur. They both created business models that are targeted at other businesses, and as such have fewer transactions at a higher dollar amount when compared with the B to C working model.

Takeaways: Which of these work models sounds the most satisfying to you? Where does your business idea fit into this picture? Will you start in one category and deliberately work your way up?

Grains of Sand

The only way that we ever accomplish anything of real enduring value is through *sustained concentrated effort.*

The author Malcolm Gladwell writes about the idea of *10,000 hours.* His theory states that people who rise to the highest levels of accomplishment in any area—be it sports, music, or any profession—do so by spending at least 10,000 hours focused on it. This equates to about 10 years of intense focus. He asserts that the geniuses we watch and admire acquired their skill not through any kind of gift from nature or from heaven, but through sheer force of sustained and focused attention. I agree with this.

Building anything, be it skill in a foreign language, ability to play the piano, or growing *a business*, is like building a mountain a few grains of sand at a time. The image here is that we are starting with nothing, and have the intention of building something of note. Something remarkable. A mountain. You add a handful of progress every time you work on your project. If you are distracted and don't continue to add on, when you eventually come back to it you will find that your progress, your mountain building, is substantially smaller. How many handfuls of attention would you need to put on a large task before you have a substantial accomplishment to look at? If you have ever worked on something or practiced something enough to become *excellent* at it, you know that it was a long process. Growing a business is also a labor-intensive process that will require an investment of sustained attention over what is likely to be a long period of time.

▓ **Note**   Being an entrepreneur—raising a business from a mere idea to the level of a successful enterprise—is a multifaceted undertaking that will only come to fruition through the coordinated and concentrated arrangement of hundreds of thousands of individual decisions and actions on your part.

As a cautionary tale, some would-be entrepreneurs that I have seen are hot and cold on actually doing the work of realizing their business ideas. One fellow in particular who I occasionally meet up with here in Austin, Texas, has substantial means at his disposal; he is from a wealthy family. He wants to be successful outside of his family's money, and has ideas that he is enthusiastic about. He puts his money and his energy into projects—up to a point. He goes all-out for a little while, and then cools off. He stops putting in the time, and the projects wilt on the vine. This is disheartening for him, and confusing for the people enlisted to help out. I think this is a problem of *intrinsic motivation*: his need is insufficient. In other words, his "why" must not be clear or sufficiently powerful enough to him.

My experience has been that when the project is right, then substantial amounts of work take care of themselves. It is not so much deciding to do it— in my case I simply find myself pushing toward the objective because I understand my "why" very clearly. Because I make sure I can connect the dots between the goals of the business and the present moment, my desire to get to the destination powers all the thousands of moving parts by itself.

Intrinsic Motivation

I make it a point to avoid the rah-rah cheerleader approach to coaching would-be entrepreneurs. I think it is a dangerous waste of time and resources for people without sufficient directed, built-in motivation to start their own businesses. Several of my good friends are extremely interested in getting people excited about starting their own businesses, and I frequently chide them about this, as I think it is a disservice.

I am not interested in convincing people that entrepreneuring is a good idea. What I am extremely interested in is helping people that already *know* they have to do it to be successful. These are *intrinsically motivated* would-be entrepreneurs that are moving forward.[2] They may need guidance, but they certainly don't need a pep talk about why they should be trying to build something. These folks are the ones that I like to spend my time coaching and assisting. Helping this group to efficiently get their ideas out is more useful to society than trying to convince otherwise passive people that they should get out there and take a chance on starting a business.

The kind of short-term motivation resulting from a good pep talk is no match for the mountain-building task of going out there and doing it.

---

[2] They have a fire burning inside them that makes them move and build something. They don't need a pep talk, but occasionally they need help and advice about how to make their vision a reality.

A Vision to Guide You

If you have decided that you are going to commit to building a business, or if you are already on your way, that is fantastic. Let's do a quick exercise together that I think will help you to get more out of your entrepreneurial voyage.

Imagine a sailing ship, white and shining in the sun . . .

Imagine that you have the boat loaded with supplies and crew, all the is equipment on board, the sails are up, and you are pulling out of port, away from the safety of land.

There you are, standing at the wheel, looking out into the bright expanse ahead. Now I will ask you a deceptively simple question: Where are you going? Are you just going *out*? Many entrepreneur sailors do just this—they head out to try to see what they can see. Inevitably, everyone in business is doing this to some extent—leaving a measure of safety and certainty behind in favor of self-determination and the excitement of finding out *what will happen*. You have to leave port and throw yourself into the wind and currents to see what you can see, find what you can find.

However, if "sailing" is the beginning and end of your strategy, you might discover problems along the way that would have been unnecessary and avoidable. What will you use as a compass? How will you interpret what your compass tells you? What decisions will be made, and on what basis?

As you leave port, which direction are you going to head in? If you are not sure, you might head south one day and north the next. Are you out on this vessel to get somewhere? If so, where? And how will you know when you get there?

I suggest that the most successful entrepreneur-sailors absorb themselves in every moment of the sailing; enjoying it for everything that it is worth. And they couple this *kinetic mental absorption* with a guiding vision. This vision sees them in a beautiful destination, a desired future place that they want to inhabit and experience.

The vision I am contemplating is a thing of rich detail, an *emotionally charged* mental construct, vibrant with colors, sounds, smells, and feelings. This destination vision is why the sailor is at sea. The vision is of the place being searched for and, in the end, even built by hand if necessary.

As the entrepreneur-sailor encounters obstacles and challenges during the voyage, this vision and all of its detail serves as a beacon to inform them of which way feels right. *Are we heading south or north? Are we running fast along the coast with the prevailing wind, or tacking against it?* The vision guides those decisions. It is this vision that will also eventually inform the realization that the *destination has been reached.* The voyage, as all things, will come to an end someday—the vision will guide you to the place you want to be when you disembark from the boat and begin your next chapter.

No matter what kind of business you are starting, be it an Internet, software, technology company, or anything else, a vision is something that you as the founder must provide. As an illustration of how to apply this, I am going to frame it in a simple and accessible business model: a pizza restaurant. This is a business that we all understand, so let's take a look at how *vision* applies here.

A Passion for Pizza

You are going to open a pizza restaurant. As the founder, how are you organizing your thoughts and purpose to make this restaurant all it can be? In the absence of a vision, you may open the doors to your pizza restaurant with the calculation of how many customers you need each day to break even, and then hope and plan to exceed that amount. This could be a guiding principle for you, but it is not very colorful, is it? So, how about a vision that inspires and informs your day-to-day actions and gives meaning to every step from the first day all the way out to years into the future? Here's a thought:

> *I love making pizza. I love to see people smile when they try my grandma's pizza crust recipe. I know it is better than any other in my town. I am going to use this passion to open a restaurant that will be the single most popular restaurant in the neighborhood. People will wait just to get a table every night. When the time is right I'm going to open other restaurants in other neighborhoods, which will provide the same quality and experience to our customers. For the rest of their lives, anytime my customers think "pizza" they are going to think of my restaurant.*

This is a sample narrative that can guide the entrepreneur in making many concrete decisions. Because you will do it for the love of it, you will

- Focus on quality and customer service, driving the popularity until it is standing-room only.

- Drive far past break-even or even profitable, heading to a future where there is enough capital to open other locations—yes, a pizza dynasty!

- Know what success looks like. You will also know when you *don't* have it, which will drive you to change any aspect of the business that falls short.

- Know when you are on the right track. Eventually you will be rewarded with the satisfaction that comes from seeing a *specific* dream realized.

The Bootstrap Mentality

The bootstrap mentality is the state of mind that comes from using your own cash to get your business going. Think about that for a second. When the money is your own, you can do anything with it that you want. An envelope with $10,000 could pay for a new kitchen in your house or a super-fancy vacation in the Bahamas. Or you could choose to invest it in your business. You had better be pretty damn sure of yourself if you are going to take thousands of your own dollars out of your wallet, with trembling fingers, and use that money to lease a new office, hire a new employee, or buy new equipment. This is very real and immediate stuff here.

Imagine how different it would feel if you were a manager at a big company and you had a budget of $10,000 to spend on a little project. You could easily decide to buy equipment or hire a contractor in that case—no problem, right?

Reframe that as someone knocking on your door and informing you that you need to write a check from your own bank account to cover $10,000 or $100,000 of office expenses. It feels a little less comfortable, doesn't it?

The point is that, mentally, there is a huge difference between spending your own money and spending company or investor money. My advice to you is that you should always treat investor or company money *as if it were your own* when you decide when, where, and how to spend it.

Back in the mid-1990s, I started a company called Meridian Internet Services with my business partner, Sterling. We launched this business in pure boot-strap mode, using our own cash to buy everything. We started quick and lean, and began pulling in revenue from customers in only a few months. All of this revenue was then rolled back into marketing the product. We were making money, but not enough to build the next generation of infrastructure that we needed. This meant that when we finally decided that we needed to upgrade, it meant scraping together all available cash and credit and then personally committing to doing it. Imagine two guys sitting at a fold-up card table counting pennies and nickels and wadded-up $1 bills mixed with gum wrappers and pocket lint. That was us. We knew what we wanted (new Dell rack-mount servers), but we could not afford the number of them that we needed. Being technically minded bootstrappers, we decided to build our server farm not machine by machine, but piece by piece. We ordered dual-processor motherboards, server cases, network cards, fans, everything. Saving money got downright comic when I fashioned the server-mounting rails for our database server from raw aluminum bars with a drill press in my garage. One particularly painful part of this was when we bought server RAM. The market price at that time, in the late 1990s was $1,000 per gigabyte—and we needed a lot of it. In the end, we outfitted a fleet of new servers, at a time when we had no cash to spare. The point here is that this necessity, when combined with lack of resources, and a commitment to being successful in our chosen field, gave us a deep and profound respect for every single dollar.

Later, when money was much less tight, we still clung to that ethos—not spending money unless it was really required. Even when working in much larger organizations later on, I continued to default to at least examining the least expensive way to get every job done.

The contrary point of view to this is evident all around, however. I worked for a startup some years later that spent $80,000 on customer relationship management (CRM) software that it never used (the company had bought it before I came on board). From my point of view, that $80,000 would have been enough to start and build an entire new business.

There is a balance that needs to be found, however. You should *not* default to the least expensive option all of the time. Very often, the cheapest route is not the best way. More often, you are going to need to spend money to get what you want, and what you need for your business. The task for the entrepreneur is learning how to look into the details of a purchase decision and accurately project into the future whether there will be any real value created from each and every significant expenditure—especially when you are just getting started. As success comes, or investor dollars head your way, cling to the ideal that each and every dollar is important and not to be squandered. Your investors will appreciate it and your company will benefit from it.

Impact to Your Personal Life

Starting and running a business will have a profound effect on your personal life. For many entrepreneurs, the business actually *becomes* their personal life. A new business is like a young child—it needs constant care. As with having a child, the impacts to your life are many and varied. Here are some observations from my experience that I did not necessarily understand before I got started.

Financial Strings Attached

When I started my second business, I did it with my friend Sterling. We were both surprised when my bank gave me $30,000 of credit on two credit cards—and we were not shy about using it. I was single at the time, so it was an individual decision that I did not hesitate to make. Fifteen months later, I got married. This was now a decision that had impact for my family, not just myself. The company was obligated to pay the debt back, which was an uncomfortable issue with my wife. She felt weighed down by the debt and poured the salary from her job as an IT consultant into the credit cards. It was a certifiably huge issue for us, and she is still a bit upset about it, to be honest.

In my mind, it was company debt, not hers or ours. In her mind, since it was in my name, it was our debt and it would drag us both down to the depths of the deep blue sea if we did not rid ourselves of it. In the end, we poured ourselves into the task of paying off the debt, and were then rewarded with a payback when we sold a spin-off business of our company to investors two short years later.

One clear pattern in the entrepreneurial world is that banks and traditional lending institutions are rarely, if ever, interested in backing an early-stage or small business without having an owner or principal in the company signing on the dotted line and taking personal responsibility. Just move forward expecting that banks are not going to loan you money without a personal commitment—they need somebody willing to put their butt on the line in case the worst happens later on. This is a significant barrier to starting a business, and should not be taken lightly.

Bankruptcy is a serious reality, and something that happens frequently enough to new business owners that you should consider carefully before plunging in and taking on debt.

Life on Hold

When you are starting a business you will find that many other important parts of your life are put on hold when you are in the early stages. My friends in Kansas City, who own an IT services company, are still wondering after seven years when they are finally going to get landscaping installed in the front yard of their home. Apparently it's been an embarrassing mess for years now.

They had a successful and growing business, but that business had been financially needy for years and is just now pulling them out of the debt they took on to start it. For them, it is a reminder of their sacrifice when they come home every evening and see that the front of their house remains bare, without the simple plants and flowers they have wanted for years. Simple? Yes. Important? Yes, of course it is. Little things can add up.

One entrepreneur that I know very well has spent so much time focused on building his business that he has put his social life on hold. He has deeply desired to be married and start a family since I have known him—over 17 years. That being the case, in his mind there has never been sufficient time even to give himself the opportunity to meet a girlfriend. The chain of business after business being set up has been all-consuming for him, and has taken over his life. In the month-after-month, year-after-year chase, through the emergencies, negotiations, operational problems, and everything else that his businesses demand of him, he emerged over a decade later still chasing the dream, and still single. It is not a matter of being blind to the passage of time and the sacrifice, but more that he has *constructed a mental place* where for years dating, finding a wife, and starting a family all *felt* impossible given the depths of the responsibilities he carried.

Time

First off, as an entrepreneur you don't often have to answer to other people for your personal time. You answer to yourself. This is fantastic if you are able to focus, and are internally driven to take each day's step in fulfilling your vision of a successful business. However, this can be disastrous if you are a procrastinator. Because you are not going to have the psychological pressure of somebody looking over your shoulder and telling you what to do, it is easy to lose track of what you are supposed to do. Don't let that happen.

In a traditional job, employees are expected to work from 9:00 a.m. to 5:00 p.m. with a one-hour lunch break, Monday to Friday. Vacation time will increase as the number of years with the company increases. Sound familiar? The pattern is familiar to all of us: get up in the morning, go to the office (busy time), come home (free time), and repeat the next day. Figure 1-1 shows what your free time looks like in a visual form.

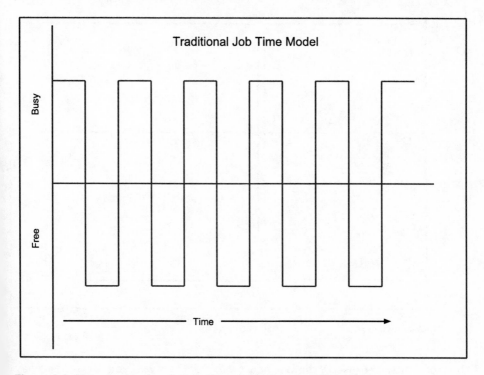

Figure 1-1. How you spend your time when working as an employee

When you work in a traditional job, it is easy to fantasize about how much free time you would have if you worked for yourself. You can show up when you want, nobody will bother you if you take a three-hour lunch break, and nobody will bother you if you go home early. That's right! Nobody will care if you don't even show up at all! Sounds fantastic!

It is true that nobody will care if you are in free-time mode when you go out on your own. The problem is that if your business is not yet fully fledged, it will shrivel up and die quicker than a tulip in Death Valley if you are not careful. The truth of the matter (and something that many first-time entrepreneurs are shocked to learn) is that most self-run businesses demand much more time than any traditional job (Figure 1-2).

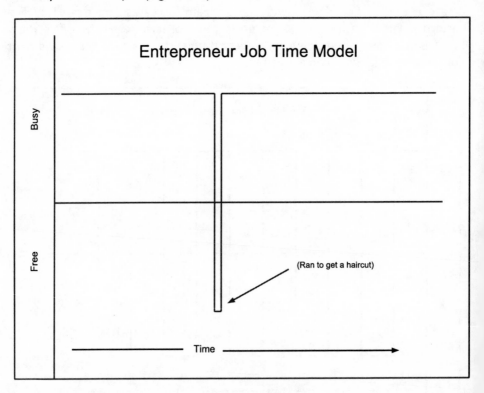

Figure 1-2. How you spend your time as an entrepreneur

The fact is that because in the beginning *the business is you*, you are never away from it. With a nine-to-five job you can *usually* turn off the noise of the office and unplug when you go home. When you own your own company, there is often no such distance to be found by returning home. If you are a full-time entrepreneur, psychological distance is very hard to achieve because you have to make the business work to pay your rent and put food on the table. It is very hard to take the afternoon off and enjoy a movie if you know that that time could be spent doing what needs to be done for the business. Always the business! The business will perpetually be waiting for you to take care of something. This will continue *until* you reach the milestones of *self-regulating* and *self-directing*, which I will talk about later in this book.

Impact to Your Health

Many people who get on the entrepreneur bandwagon often do so at the expense of their physical well-being. I know a number of businessmen who let the demands of being The Decider serve as an excuse to delay physical activity until later on—day after day. This translates into not exercising at all, and weight adding on pound by pound. What follows is the familiar refrain that "I am too busy, so there is no choice!" Bull.

Don't let your business keep you locked up. You are better off deciding to take care of yourself. Exercise and a good diet are the fuel for your body and mind. The business needs a vibrant and fit leader more than it needs that extra 90 minutes from you three times a week. Get out of the office and exercise. Find something cardiovascular and repetitive that will allow you the quiet time to reflect on your business and the market environment from the distance of a running track, hiking trail, or lap pool. The time away from the office, along with the physical stimulation, is perfect for activating your subconscious mind and triggering your creativity. The work that you were focused on in the office will come back to you with a new perspective and a new clarity if you deliberately create distance from it. Also, a healthy and vibrant CEO is more likely to interact successfully with other businesspeople. Like it or not, the CEO crowd at the highest levels tends to be healthy and athletic. Go ahead and join the club, and don't use your busy schedule as another excuse for not taking care of yourself.

Resources

Anything that is yours might end up in service of your business. The boundaries between office and home blur. Tools from the garage? They are at the business, having been used for the thing you were doing last week. Papers on the kitchen table? Those are from the marketing campaign we are putting together.

In my case, I ran an office out of my home for several years. My partner had database servers running in his spare bedroom at one point (the electricity bill went up by hundreds of dollars per month that summer). At another time, we had my business partner's garage stacked floor to ceiling with pallets of merchandise that we had manufactured in China. That garage was so full that he was worried that the foundation of his house was going to crack.

So, impact to your personal life can be wide and varied. In fact, seeing the wide range of areas in this discussion, we can come to the conclusion that being an entrepreneur is apt to affect every aspect of your life. This is not something that you can easily compartmentalize. When you are fully committed to a business, it will touch and affect every aspect of your life—your health, wealth, relationships, and everything in between. For those of you that are intrinsically motivated—that have to do it—it won't matter. If this list of costs and pain points is off-putting for you, then that's a good thing. Much better to find out from a book and decide that it's worth avoiding than to commit to The Life and realize that it's a bad fit.

Core Lessons

Some things are universal. In life and in business, some things pass the test of time and seem to come up again and again as relevant and useful to know. Required knowledge.

Core Lessons is a collection of ideas on building a business—ideas that I see as universal. If this were a biology book, here is where the author would thoughtfully point out that all life requires water and energy to survive. This chapter will survey some universally relevant truths that you can apply to your business no matter whether you are in Silicon Valley, in Tokyo, or on Mars. This is also where you will find out some of the more painful details of how I have screwed up, been blindsided, or otherwise been subjected to a stone-fisted kibosh or two.

These core lessons are the kind of business rules that are of über-importance—the kind of things that I would carve in stone and erect before the townspeople. As I emphasize the importance of carefully constructing a set of "frames" with which to view your business, you will find a number of them here that will inform your decisions as an entrepreneur. As basic as some of these points sound, they may not be as intuitive and automatic as they should be; even seasoned and experienced entrepreneurs that have read advance versions of this book have commented on how a few of these points were things that they had not thought about explicitly before, but ended up agreeing with wholeheartedly.

Basics Win Ball Games

The most successful businesses are those that master the basic transactions of their market and execute them with reliability and excellence.

Identify what the *core operations* are for your market, and what the constituent parts of those operations are. Then ask yourself if you are executing the mundane details as well as you are capable of. "Winning" is very often the result of focusing on the little details, and then doing them well again and again.

Consider this: the difference between wild success and complete failure may be as small as a 3 percent difference in your performance, run out over a period of years. With this in mind, the little things start to look more and more important.

Excellence starts with basics. If the basic operations of your business are not being handled, then the sexy new stuff, new opportunities, and exciting "next" things will mean much less to you. You have to get the basic current operations down and running well before you spend too much energy grasping for the next big thing.

No Partial Credit

A critical difference between being an employee and running your own business is the idea that there's *no partial credit* given for your efforts. When you are working for a company, in good times and not-so-good times, you can count on a paycheck. If you do your job well (or even not so well), you get a paycheck. If the company fails to meet its sales figures, or misses a product launch window, everyone still gets paid (so long as the company does not go out of business). The company assumes the burden of providing security for its employees, so in many ways the absolute necessity to perform is present, but not pointed. The entrepreneur does not usually have that level of security.

My business partner Sterling often lamented that it was all or nothing with our work. On numerous projects, we would only make money if we got *everything* lined up in perfect fashion. If we got 95 percent done (which is normally an "A" in school and most other cases), we would still be in the same state as if we had just sat and watched *Matlock* reruns on the USA Network for the last ten months.

In one case, our company made a play to outrun the competitors by developing an automated sales engine that would post products such as books and DVDs to online marketplaces such as eBay and Amazon. The system would fetch real-time inventory information from supply warehouses across the United States, automatically post and audit online sales listings, and communicate with online payment services, banks, and an in-house fulfillment process—including an automated packing robot. Wow! The problem was that huge chunks of this operation were an all-or-nothing proposition. That is to say, the company would benefit not a whit until the whole darn thing was finished, tested, plugged in, and primed with money to start the goods flowing. 99 percent done? Big whoop, because we still can't use it. In this case, our normal operations, because they were mostly manual and time intensive, were sewing up 100 percent of available resources most of the time. We were robbing Peter to pay Paul to get more development done, because it meant transactions in progress now, and existing customers had to be deprioritized (just a tad) for us to even look at system enhancements (Figure 2-1).

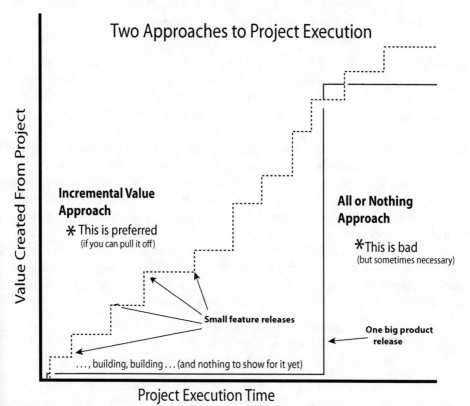

Figure 2-1. "All or nothing" is the wrong way to structure deliverables: Value should be earned throughout your projects

Back in 1999, our company Meridian Internet Services was running several operations at once, including a group of branded social networking sites, developing proprietary search engine optimization systems (getting web sites ranked well on search engines), running powerful search engine marketing campaigns (efficiently paying for traffic across the Web), and growing a spin-off geographic data business. With a social media business, one of the clear value propositions is that you have lots of different kinds of people visiting you and sharing information with you and with each other. Often, this is potentially valuable information that could help you to market to them in an effective way. Years before Google AdWords appeared, we designed a business called BannerEdge (back when banner ads were important) that would allow a dynamic auction of advertising based on deep criteria matching of the people that the advertiser wanted to target. This was an ambitious project and had profound implications for connecting advertisers with very specific groups of people. Mathematically, the project could have made us a great deal of money. (That "could have" in the previous sentence sounds ominous, doesn't it?)

Brainstorming and development of this project was underway, and we invested months of time. We developed new database structures, new user interfaces, and dynamic auction algorithms from scratch. These things take time—and in our case took a lot of time. While our social networking business continued to grow, from a development perspective it was put on hold so we could follow the opportunity for a much bigger success with the new real-time auction-advertising model. A whole year of heads-down development work was eventually put into this project. But it never saw the light of day. The social networking business hit an iceberg, and the raison d'être for BannerEdge went away. The opportunity cost of that lost time was staggering; it turned into a full year of effort for our company to be flushed down the proverbial … ahem … washbasin. Also mentally devastating was the fact that all of the thought, work, and dreams associated with the brave new world of marketing that we envisioned disappeared into the dustbin of history without so much as one user seeing it, and without it ever making us a single, solitary dollar.

The lesson for me here was that this project took a lot of time. It was ambitious. But it was also not going to make any incremental revenue for us until it was completed, released into the wild, and connected with customers.

What could we have done differently, you might wonder? Perhaps we could have postponed the targeting algorithms and real-time auction and just made an interface where buyers could create ads and sell them to our population of users. With this base, we could have theoretically begun a revenue stream and learned about how media buyers behave. From that we could have added on our additional game-changing features one at a time. Hindsight is one hell of a painful thing sometimes, isn't it?

I recently had the opportunity to meet some development team leaders from Google, and when they described their product strategy, it was similarly structured: Define the smallest piece of functionality that would be even potentially useful for customers, build it, and then ship it. Use that experience and user feedback to develop the feature set as you decide what is next from a feature standpoint.

Takeaway: Structure your projects to provide incremental value as you go.

Diversify

Diversification can keep you alive. *Diversification* is a buzzword in financial markets for a reason. It makes a critical difference when things don't go as planned … because things frequently don't go as planned.

Common Single Points of Failure

When you fly in an airliner, you can just sit back, relax, and enjoy the ride. You don't need to worry very much about crashes, mechanical failures, or other problems because a lot of careful attention is paid by the engineers to make sure that when you set off from one city to another, you will get there intact and happy. They accomplish this task firstly by engineering the hell out of the components, and they install redundant mechanisms for all vital systems on every aircraft. Your business is very much like that airliner: you build it to get you somewhere. It is designed to carry you and your team to that destination in one piece, preferably without crashing, having mechanical failures, or encountering critical problems.

Just like the aircraft engineers at Boeing, you should identify your key systems, and then add redundancies to them. The purpose being that when failures do occur (and they will), you will reduce the severity and consequence of that event from "Passengers and crew, brace for impact!" to a less dramatic "Stewardess, that bump spilled my coffee!"

Here are some single points of failure that have been significant in my businesses.

A Single Distribution Channel

When the media sales company that I was part owner of was faced with a change in policy with its PayPal transaction capability, our primary sales channel (eBay.com) suddenly fell off the radar screen. This meant closing our doors. The company had known for over two years that it needed to diversify, but the development and marketing resources to do so were not sufficient to keep pace with surging real-time business demands *and* open up other sales channels at the same time. In an unrelated point, I was a passive shareholder and could not force the executive team to heed the advice: diversify! Such single points of failure had come near to killing the business on at least three different occasions. To continue the aircraft analogy, it was a known design flaw of the aircraft, and eventually the pilots, crew, and passengers paid a high price for it.

A Single Key Employee

This person has unique knowledge required to do your business. What will you do if he moves on, or (in business parlance) gets hit by a bus? Don't wait to find out—hire more talent and train them to know what your key guy knows.

In my current role, I am constantly on the task of making sure my team members are redundant from one to the other. When an imbalance comes into being where one guy holds too much information that others don't have, I either cross-train them or request budget to hire another team member to provide coverage.

A Single Channel

Depending on one source for your leads and business can be a big risk too. If you depend on being on the first page of Google for most of your business, you are going to have problems if/when you are no longer at the top of the search results. Build diversification into your plan. These days, Google is the primary source of traffic and sales for many online businesses. What would you do if that part of your customer acquisition strategy was cut in half, or disappeared entirely? That is a tough question to answer, but in finding an answer (even in part) you will be making large steps toward disaster-proofing your operation, while adding more business in the process. Diversification will mean more business in good times and survivability in bad times.

An Outsized Large Client

If your company depends disproportionately on one client such as Wal-Mart, then you are clearly at risk. A simple change in that company's mindset or strategy could leave you in a dire situation without notice and without recourse. Diversify your channels to include other clients if possible.

Sometimes it *makes sense* to focus on one large client, though. A good friend of mine has a banking services business with one major client that provides over 90 percent of his transaction volume. We discussed diversification many times, and his conclusion was that it is extremely difficult, if not impossible to diversify in his case. After a couple of years of worry, his response to that single point of failure was to double down and increase his volume with the client. He decided that his best path was to make sure that the client is as dependent on him as he is on them. This way of addressing the single point of failure has worked well for him so far: profits and volume are up. Now that he has stopped worrying about finding other customers, he is able to focus more of his attention on that one customer and lock in that relationship. Meanwhile, since he is consciously aware of the risk, he is banking as much profit as possible as a hedge against a future fluctuation in the fortunes or requirements of that single large customer.

Takeaway: Identify single points of failure. Find a way to manage them before they bite you in a way that you can't recover from. I have seen entire companies and years of work lost to this. Don't let it happen to you.

Specific Intention

In business, it is really important to have a specific intention behind everything you do. If you are going to spend money on marketing, what specifically are you trying to accomplish with the investment? If you're going to hire a new employee, in what specific ways do you plan to benefit from having another person on staff? If you're going to invest money and buy new software, in what ways do you think your business will be more efficient or in what ways will value be created?

An analogy that I like to use is playing pool. Most of us have played the game at one time or another. The first time I ever really played was in college. I occasionally found it frustrating trying to figure out how to make the balls do precisely what I wanted, and I could succumb to the temptation to just hit the cue ball as hard as possible, thinking that at least something would end up in a pocket. The fact of the matter is that just hitting the ball hard in the absence of a specific intention is one of the worst options available. As a beginner, in the process of evaluating the best ways to win, the just-hit-it-hard strategy is always there, waiting, as a fallback option when you don't know what else to do. In my case, however, it did not take long to realize that if I wanted any reliable chance of getting what I wanted, I really needed to have a specific intention: eight ball in the corner pocket.

In business there are lots of similar situations. For example, experience has shown me that you can throw money at anything. You can buy an expensive phone system. You can purchase new furniture. You can hire extra salespeople. There's no end to the ways that you can invest money in your business. I want to reiterate that point:

> *There is no end to the ways in which you can invest money in your business.*

A corollary to this is that most of the ways in which you can invest money in your business are not going to have a clear positive outcome. You have to be very selective of where every dollar goes in your operation. That selectivity comes from specifically defining your intentions before you move forward with any investment.

Often, when you get into an honest evaluation of an investment decision, you will find you don't need what you thought you did, or that you can function at 100 percent with much less than you thought at first blush.

A Waste of Cash, Time, and Energy

At a dot-com startup where I was an executive, the investors behind the operation had a history of getting personally involved with decision-making and day-to-day operations. On one occasion, they decided to purchase a $100,000 phone system. That thing was complicated. It probably seemed cool to imagine what such a system could do, but it was completely impractical and way too expensive to be justified for the still-money-losing operation. This is an example of just hitting the cue ball as hard as possible and hoping something good happens.

The business need was simple: to have a phone with a voice mailbox for each employee. Period. What was chosen was a corporate-level, multi-city, computer-controlled, integrated phone system with dedicated T1 Internet connectivity. It was also a system that was prone to breaking and that nobody on staff understood how to operate. The funny thing about investments like this is that the costs aren't just in the sticker price. The operational cost was several thousand dollars a month for just the dedicated Internet connecting the offices. It cost us money every time we needed to change the system because we had to hire a specialized consultant to come onsite. These guys were hard to find, difficult to get to answer our phone calls, and outrageously expensive when they did show up. Another hidden expense was lost productivity, when employees and engineering staff were trying to get this thing to work, instead of designing products. Lost calls and unanswered voice mails were yet more cost points for us.

Instead of pursuing an inexpensive yet adequate solution, the investor who made the purchase decision felt a need for a "phone system." What followed next was an emotional response to some telco marketing materials that painted a picture of business success and the required infrastructure behind it, which went along the lines of, "Imagine multiple cities combined on one private security network, with intelligent phone message routing, and with productive, smiling, employees happily routing customer after customer to one another on the BizNet 2000[1] phone system."

This is a much sexier vision than what we probably actually needed. If it had been planned out in advance (in the absence of the sales propaganda), we could have functioned well enough with a central toll-free number connecting to a receptionist desk with an answering system. Sales people and other staff could have a POTS (plain-old telephone system) line or a cell phone. Is this perfect? No. Would it work? Yes. The actual best-case scenario is probably somewhere between the POTS solution and the BizNet 2000, but the guidance of specific intentions could have led to a saner solution:

---

[1] Fictional name.

- Customers should be able to reach the company by phone, and the company should be able to respond professionally.

- Each staff member should have a phone with voice mail.

Specific intentions, defined before an investment is made, guide how the investment is made, when it is made, how it is executed, and how it is evaluated along the way. This set of specific intentions, if laid out and pursued, could have saved the company a lot of money.

Backing Up the Truck

Recently, we had a meeting where the team was discussing what we were going to do to implement Facebook more centrally on our site. The discussion was on where and how Facebook would be added to our user experience. I had joined the meeting late, and was interested in finding out what the point was. I asked that we "back up the truck a bit," and figure out the answer to "Why?" This is closely related to having a specific intention.

"*Why* are we adding Facebook to the site? What specific intention do we have, and how will that be reached by the options we are discussing?"

The question seemed to take everyone by surprise. In fact, nobody was able to articulate *why* we were going to integrate Facebook more centrally into our user experience. Would we get more users? No. Would we get more money, as a business? No. I took a stab at it by saying, "While we don't have any specific intention to get more customers or more money, we believe that it is useful to experiment with Facebook integration as a means to gain more experience in social media, and to gather data on whether or not users will engage with our brand in more meaningful ways through this tool set."

This specific intention, shared between team members, was useful in that it framed the exercise as a reconnaissance mission as opposed to a fundamental reimagining of our brand experience. The engineers and creatives were then able to understand how much gravity (or lack thereof) was at play with the project. As it was, users did not really want to opt into that tool set when we deployed it, and it was removed from the site entirely within a few weeks.

Takeaway: When starting any project, always ask yourself and the people involved to describe the specific intention of the effort. Beyond saying "do this," clearly describing the desired outcome will help you to ensure that value is being created, and that everyone has clear insight into the thought process behind the actions they are taking.

How to Determine the Demand of the Market

This is basic. Anybody who reads this will say, "I already know this." Be that as it may, even seasoned executives can forget this from time to time.

The exercise: Identify the total set of all potential customers, and the expected transaction value for each one per unit of time. Then calculate the percentage of them you think you can reach with your marketing message. Follow up by estimating how many will actually pull the trigger and pay you their hard-earned cash (Figure 2-2).

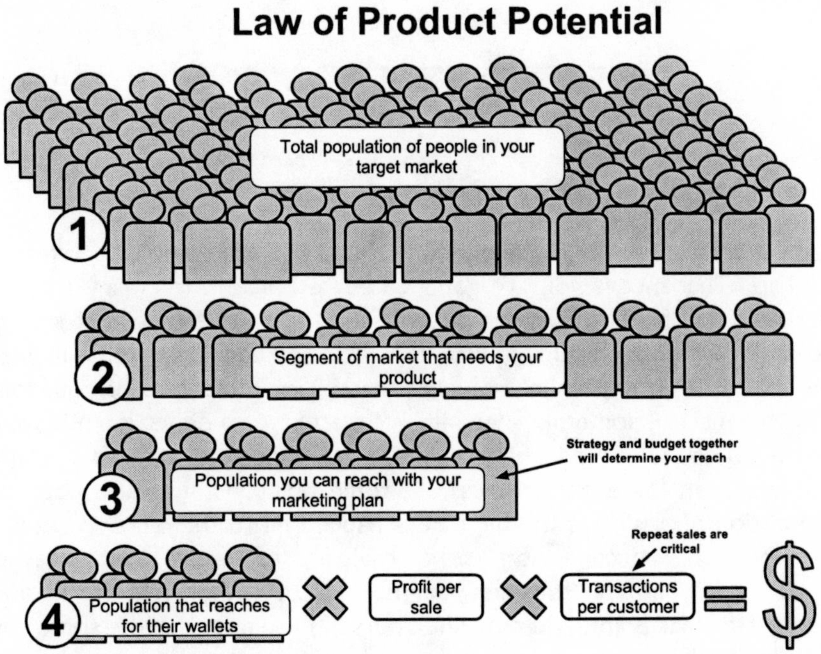

Law of Product Potential

1 Total population of people in your target market

2 Segment of market that needs your product

3 Population you can reach with your marketing plan
Strategy and budget together will determine your reach

4 Population that reaches for their wallets ✕ Profit per sale ✕ Transactions per customer = $
Repeat sales are critical

Figure 2-2. The law of profit potential

A useful way to apply this rule when analyzing a business opportunity is to ask yourself how much money is in the entire market for the product or service. In other words, how much would you make if you were able to take 100 percent of the transaction volume that is available? This first analytical step concerns the market opportunity.

The next step is to ask honestly how much you can expect to capture in the next year, and then in the next two years, and so on. Basic. I will often "chunk down" and ask this same question about incremental changes to an existing product. "If we modify our product by adding A and B, how much more sales can we really expect to capture?"

This idea is important as heck because it can help you to identify the good ideas and prevent you from chasing the silly ones. Going ahead and doing this exercise *every time* you want to consider a new product or a product change is a *must do*. It will add clarity to what might seem at the gut level to make sense, but on closer observation isn't worth pursuing.

Make Yourself Obsolete

When you start out, as the founder of a business you are going to be wearing multiple hats. That means you are going to be responsible for many areas of your business, and be The Decider on everything from the important stuff to the necessary but time-consuming little things. In the beginning, you will likely become a hands-one expert in multiple areas of your business. If you don't know how to manage something, you are going to have to either learn it yourself, or hire someone to do it for you. Hiring out for certain tasks is a natural phase of evolution for every business. At some point in the future you may have the option of posing as the big CEO, chauffeured to the office every day, known to ominously occupy a big leather chair and to steeple your fingertips under your chin while you consider your further plans for world domination. Until you get to that point, you may find yourself needing to handle some customer support calls, vacuum floors, and even fix your computer network when it goes down.

Advertising agent, marketing and product planner, security expert, customer support representative, business trend prognosticator, contract negotiator, legal document writer, intellectual property monitor, window cleaner, paper clip buyer, furniture assembler, utility bill payer—these are some of the many hats you may wear.

Figure 2-3 illustrates a trend. The trend is going from 100 percent you to a small percent you. This trend line represents a process that you have heard of before: the process of *delegation*.

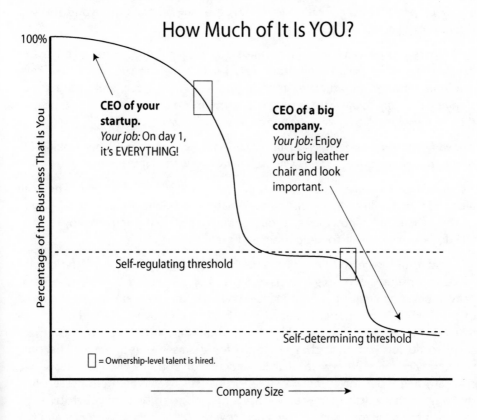

Figure 2-3. Trend line representing delegation

Delegation means

- Hiring the right people

- Training them to understand the business (start with why and then work your way up to what and how)

- Gradually giving up control, providing feedback along the way

- Empowering your employees to make decisions and to make mistakes

For key team members, it means connecting performance with compensation: equity or profit sharing. This is key to progressing up to and beyond the *self-determining threshold*.

Be prepared to delegate as your business gets bigger. You are going to *need* to delegate. Look forward to this and regard it as a sign of success. If you have run your business month after month, and year after year, and you are not trending strongly toward delegating more and more important tasks to others, then you may need to take a hard look at what it is you are doing.

Knowing that you are going to need to delegate, you should be looking for quality people *from the first day you even think about starting a business.*

As an employee, it may seem that employers have all of the power. They can hire and fire at will, and they can direct what the employees do. The other side of the coin is very interesting, though: employers *need* good employees and will do what they must to keep them and grow them.

To attract and keep the kind of talent that can actually take over the corner office and make the strategic decisions that will be needed to keep the company in business without your guidance, you will need to break out of the mold of pure salary-based compensation. This kind of employee will eventually demand a bonus or equity-based compensation that will properly incentivize them to do for you what they could do for themselves (go out and become your competitor). Otherwise, that key person or persons will likely leave the company and work for somebody else, or just start their own businesses. It is the way of the world that you will have to empower them through training, exposing them to your knowledge, and provide operational experience and the ability to make, and learn from, mistakes. All of these things create confidence and competence. The qualities of confidence and competence in executive functions require you to recategorize these types of employees into an executive class that shares directly in organizational success. Not doing this will mean that you'll lose their talent and knowledge. That puts the future of the company at risk, because it takes years to groom such employees for the roles that you have in mind. This being said, even if you compensate them at an executive level, there is no guarantee that they won't leave anyway. Building a personal rapport and a culture that supports emotional buy-in, and providing a vision of what the business means, and where it is going, are key to increasing your chances of success.

A cornerstone of your plan should be, in most cases, to make yourself obsolete. Why should this be? Part of the appeal of being an entrepreneur (for most people) is being able to call the shots and to be master of your domain. This is truly part of being a business owner/operator. However, this becomes somewhat less rosy if you fall into the trap where instead of owning a business, the business ends up owning you. This inevitably happens at the outset of your business. The goal is to grow the business, its team, and its processes to the point where it can become self-regulating at the least and self-directing at best.

The Self-Regulating Business

A *self-regulating* business is one where the principal (you) can unplug for hours or days or weeks at a time without the business falling apart. On the long road to making yourself obsolete, this is the first big and impressive milestone. I define *self-regulating* to be the stage at which you, the founder of your business, can lie dormant in a hammock on Fiji (with mai tai in hand) for two weeks— without e-mail or phone—and be confident that your business will still be happily humming when you return. Self-regulating businesses have competent and empowered employees who know the day-to-day operations and do not need your explicit direction to perform them.

The staff knows how to respond to most situations, and it is empowered to make the day-to-day decisions required to keep all of the wheels turning and the customers happy. It will probably take years of work to develop a self-regulating team (see Figure 2-3 again), and it should be one of the primary intermediate goals you set for yourself. You should begin thinking about it as soon as you get out of business infancy and prove that your business model is workable, and begin to carve out an economic niche in which you can prosper.

The Self-Determining Business

Getting your business to the *self-determining* level is the ultimate delegation accomplishment, because it means you have found, hired, and trained a staff that knows the daily operations, and you have also installed managers who know the big picture—and are prepared to make the long-term strategic decisions that you have been making all this time. In terms of what this means to you, it means you can come into the office and work, or go to Fiji (again), or, most importantly, sell the company if you want to. If you plan to sell your business at some future point (having an *exit strategy*), you being obsolete will make the business more attractive to potential buyers. Why would anybody buy a business that will end up having a required component (the previous owner) missing after the purchase?

You Will Need More Money Than You Think

How much capital you have when you start out is a critical piece of your survivability. Make sure you have enough to get started, and to survive a few mistakes after your business is open. Know ahead of time the following things. Problems will arise that you did not anticipate—problems that will cost money to solve. Things will generally take longer than you thought to get going. Expenses will likely be higher than you estimated. If you plan with this bias, you will have more survivability built into your plan. So don't embark on your venture until you have some reserve cash available to help in a disaster. Identify sources of credit that you can tap if needed as a last-ditch, break-glass-in-case-of-emergency backup plan. Here are some examples:

- Series B (or C or D) financing (more rounds of financing means less value left for you)[2]

- Line of credit at the bank (potentially dangerous)

- A rich uncle (also potentially dangerous!)

- Credit cards (even more dangerous)

---

[2] *Series B* indicates the second round of formal investor funding in a company. The sequential naming traditionally follows the alphabet: Series A, Series B, Series C, and so on.

Use suppliers as a source of credit whenever possible. In an online retail business where I was a partner, this was a boon; wholesale companies would extend credit to cover cost of goods on 30- or 60-day terms. That meant being able sell and generate revenue and pay later. Magic.

Design your business to start making money quickly if possible, and don't start spending money like you are a big business until you are a big business. Get something out the door and generating cash as fast as possible so that revenue can cover many of your expenses early on.

Active Iteration

In a meeting of the engineers and creative folk, I was recently reviewing the fantastic success we had in growing our product portfolio and reaching nearly 5 million users per month. I dangerously mixed metaphors and summed up our accomplishment by saying "our secret sauce is that we know how to dance."

What I meant was that we execute idea after idea for communicating our value and getting more customers. In so doing, we rapidly iterate over each concept with minimal up-front effort, while tweaking for performance. Some of these ideas are winners, which we invest more time in. Some are not clear winners, but don't take a lot of time, so we let them be. Some other mechanisms that we try just perform badly, so we withdraw them. This is a dance. As we do it we find that over the passage of time, the center of gravity of our operation changes, step by step in the (otherwise hidden) evolving direction of the market. The fact that we gather data on many different strategies simultaneously gives us the information we need to act smart and choose the best options. In the absence of multiple simultaneous outreaches into the market, we would be less likely to perform well. It would be a matter of chance when what we were doing worked (or didn't). We increase the odds of success proportionate to the number of things we try. Key is that each of these efforts is relatively small in terms of resources employed.

A core strategy for finding and capitalizing on a business model that works is to *actively iterate* through variations of ideas and strategies to connect with customers and fulfill their needs. It is important to always keep feelers out in the market for changes. Adapt as the market changes to avoid drastic and painful adjustments later. This means building in feedback mechanisms to keep you connected to the pulse of the market, as well as a set of measures that will help you to detect change as it happens and before it becomes any kind of threat to your survival.

Here are some examples of feedback mechanisms:

- Talking to your customers

- Tracking classic performance metrics such as sales, visitors, cost per lead, cost per sale, and inventory levels.

- Tracking the performance of each marketing source (e.g., separate phone numbers for different campaigns)

Your data collection is only useful if it alters or has the potential to alter your decision-making. Clearly, the most relevant and meaningful data in the world is useless to you if you do not have a willingness to allow it to change how you do things. If you are going to go to the effort to gather data, couple that with a commitment to listen to it and to act on what it tells you.

Let's boil this down by looking at Figure 2-4. There are three iterative phases of operation for a business strategy: exploration, refinement, and repetition.

Active Iteration

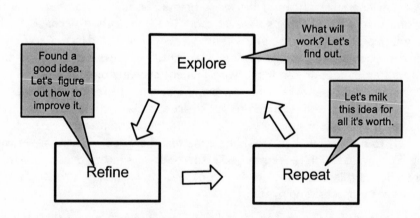

A healthy business should run this cycle numerous times in parallel

Figure 2-4. The phases of forming a business strategy

Exploration is when you are not sure what will work. You are putting out feelers to find what the market will respond to. *Refinement* is when you have found a way of touching your customers that has promise, and you are tweaking it to make it sharper and better. *Repetition* is when you have explored and refined, and hit the point of diminishing returns on tweaking a particular activity. Once you have something that works, you repeat it for as long as the market will bear it. Successful businesses are based around this cycle, sometimes running dozens of such cycles in parallel.

■ **Note** Your business is like a living organism. If you understand it as such, and treat it as such, you will play Charles Darwin and search for opportunities to evolve by pushing the boundaries of what you understand, and what you are capable of doing. You will treat this evolutionary research and adaptation as a core component of your operations.

A *feedback loop* is a system in which data is collected at regular intervals, and that data is used to correct or alter the conduct of your business at regular intervals. This is the same type of system that governs all living creatures, both great and small. If it is good enough for nature, it is good enough for your business. Beyond that, I would say that multiple feedback loops are required for you to be successful in any business venture that has even a medium level of complexity.

The result of active feedback loops, and general feedback from all sources, will likely be a series of stages of evolution over time. This is adaptation, just as a living organism will adapt to its environment as the environment changes. Pay attention to two rules here:

- Avoid doing something today just because it was what you did yesterday. Be open to changing any process or aspect of your operation if needed.

- Experiment with low-risk feelers into new and untried activities. Set aside some of your capital to dedicate to novel gestures that can connect you to your existing market or altogether new markets in ways that you have not tried before. This is very important. Constant experimentation is the cornerstone strategy for moving beyond survival and becoming a standout success among your peers in any kind of business. You will find business ideas that fail, some that break even, and a few that will *really work*. The best ones will eventually become core to your operation, while some things that you do today will eventually become obsolete and you will stop doing them altogether. This is fundamental.

Takeaway: Search for low-cost opportunities to try to connect with your customers. Gather data to improve your business, but do not make the effort to gather data on a process or facet of your business if you know it will not affect your decision-making.

Always Get a Contract

When I look back to when I started my first real company in my early twenties, I was much the same as I am now. I am certainly older now and some would say wiser. Part of that wisdom is that at least some of my boyish naiveté has been replaced by an understanding of how people can be downright unfriendly to one another. I hate to bring this up, but I can't paint things over when it comes to this topic. It's something we must discuss.

From my perspective, it comes down to psychology. Whether or not people are willing to treat each other with respect, honesty, and dignity is dependent to a large extent on whether they feel any personal identification with the other person and whether they have established and maintained a proper psychological contract. Getting along means maintaining an "us" mentality.

The problem is that even good people can fall out of this "us" paradigm very easily. Things happen, and communication is a very difficult thing to maintain.

Especially when money is on the line, relationships and understandings can be stretched or torn apart.

Take the following scenario as an example. You start a business with a business partner. Later, the business has problems. You think they are his fault and thus feel comfortable telling anybody who will listen that he is not the person he used to be. Your partner meanwhile thinks the problems arose because you are always out of town, traveling with your wife to Rolling Stones concerts. What we have here are people who, through a natural course of events, have come to a place where they no longer see eye to eye. Who is right? It depends on where you are standing, as both appear 'right' from their own vantage points. This imaginary scenario is a simple illustration of how one-time friends can come to a cold place where they want to sue the living daylights out of one another.

In another instance, a good friend of mine earned a share in a company over several years, to be fully vested upon its sale. A great deal of work went into building the business into something worthy of acquisition, which eventually came. When the sale was completed, no mention of the equity vesting was ever offered. When he brought it up, he was told that due to the fact that it was an asset sale and not a sale of the actual company, there would be no payout. The fine print here is that the company was never 'sold' per se, but all the assets were—leaving the company only a name on a piece of paper with no residual value. That's great, isn't it? No two ways about it, the people who had worked and struggled for the company felt ... how should I say this in a polite manner? Well, that they had not been treated fairly. In this case, he did have a contract, which was plain and to the point, but not written in a way that fully protected him in the situation at hand. He had thought that a big contract was unnecessary because the owners were "good folks" that looked him straight in the eye at meeting after meeting for years—and had agreed to equity sharing.

I can only imagine what the owners of the company who got millions of dollars in the transaction were thinking. Mind reading is a dangerous thing, but they likely felt that they always treat people fairly and that the employees in question had actually failed to deliver in some way.

Everybody considers themselves to be justified in their actions. All of this is a matter of perspective.

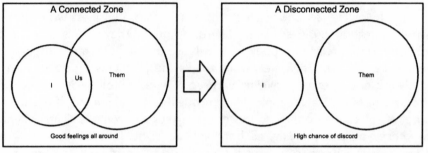

Figure 2-5. Time and lack of effective communication can lead to problems that nobody wants

Another recent instance comes to mind. I met a gentleman in Albany, New York who is a lobbyist working with the state government. He, in his suit and tie and with his youthful enthusiasm, is the only employee of a small firm, and he works under the owner. This young man works for $200 per week. His story is that he is willing to work for less than the minimum wage because the company is going to grow, and his boss "takes care of him," as he put it. The boss buys him lunch most days and gives him an extra Hamilton or two when he needs it. In listening to this, I started to get a bit agitated. I asked the question, "Does your boss *need* you in order to continue his business? Are you critical?" The answer was a decided yes. Furthermore, since the boss "takes care of him," my friend believes that he is going to be taken care of when the business grows into something bigger. My advice to him was, "Get a contract." Directly communicate that the only way to move forward is to trade "fair value for fair value."

I told him this, "You should expect an equity share to compensate for the lack of a living wage, and the fact that you are critical to the business." I also told him that he should directly ask for it in a fair, level-headed, transaction-minded way. The likely outcome otherwise will be that the young man diligently puts in his time, grows the business, and then gets handed his walking papers when he asks for any special consideration later on. Never count on your boss agreeing with you that your effort was critical to the success that created the business, after all is said and done—it is not going to be visible to him in the same way it is to you.

Peter, a good friend of mine put it succinctly when he said, "Emotion has no place in business." Clearly, people, as emotional beings bring emotion to everything they do, but he means that you should lock down your under-standings and agreements in a contract or written form so that the ambiguity of emotional decision making can be held in check.

So, I say this to anyone who will listen:

1. Never rely on abstract ideas like "good feelings" or beliefs like "they are great people" or "I feel like I can trust him" in business. These are important things, but they are not sufficient by themselves for forming the basis of real and reliable business relationships. Assume that the worst will happen.

2. Get a contract to define roles, responsibilities, ownership, and financial details for any aspect of the business that has value.

3. Have your contracts reviewed by an attorney that represents you as an individual—distinct from the company.

4. Remember that nothing changes things like money. If your business be-comes valuable, you will be thankful for having worked out everything between the people involved well in advance.

Create value together with your partners and build something that benefits everyone in powerful ways, but put a mechanism together that protects you.

Watch Intellectual Property

Intellectual property is important. It is easy to get in trouble when you don't remember this. With the quick availability of information, images, video, opinions, software, and any other kind of human output that you can imagine on the Internet, it is easy to forget that much of this content is owned by people or companies that are serious about protecting it.

By 1999, we were running a whole network of online sites similar to Match.com. On one of the home pages, one of our guys did a rework of the layout, with large images of happy people that would randomly change out each time you visited the page. The layout looked great and people liked it. Our conversion of traffic from visitor to member went up a small percentage with the new design.

A few weeks after this new interface went live, we got a phone call, followed by a letter from a legal firm: "You are using our unlicensed images—remove them or be taken to court." They sent a detailed list of the "borrowed" images that were being used on our site. The guy who had redone the site had decided not to properly license the images he was using and instead just downloaded them and put them in the layout. We were looking at potentially thousands of dollars in attorney fees and civil penalties in court, so what looked like a time- and money-saving shortcut ended up taking executive time to respond in emergency mode, as well as a potential capital-draining sortie into an unnecessary and unproductive legal quagmire. Not good at all. I would have fired the guy who did it, but he was my business partner. Bad boy! As it was, we were able to diffuse the situation. We immediately removed the images and were lucky that they were not interested in pursuing the matter.

In an exploratory venture, we started a business producing products in China and selling them nationwide in the United States. Our first trans-Pacific freight container of products ended up being unsellable because of a claim of trademark infringement from a competitor. I will never forget what our contact at the Chinese manufacturer said: "We just make the product. It's not our responsibility to check and make sure it's legal to sell it in your country." Touché. Just imagine a warehouse full of product, and not being able to sell it. A word printed on the stuff was registered as a trademark by somebody else. It hurt. A lot. We ended up letting the competitor send over a truck and load up every last crate and take it from us. At least they paid for the shipping. We felt grateful to be done with it.

The lesson is this: intellectual property is important. Avoid any easy or obvious landmines, but remember that if you are visible enough, people will come after you whether you have done anything wrong or not. Just have a good lawyer and be ready to invest money in your defense.

Control the Money

Don't depend on any one connection point to your customers (or their money) too heavily. Don't depend on any one mechanism (like a single credit card merchant account) to funnel your money.

If you have money flowing into a merchant account, or another payment account that third-party agencies have access to, never leave any amount of money there. Always put it in another account as soon as each deposit is made.

Back in the days when we were running the social networking firm, we charged around $30 per month for people to join. (This business was very similar to Match.com.) After a year or so, we had nearly a million registered users—not all of them paying—but only after a long process of gathering members a few at a time at first, then by the hundreds, and then by the thousands per day.

This business model was based on the concept of *rebilling*. We would charge a new member for an initial membership, and then in subsequent months the same amount would automatically be rebilled on their credits cards until they cancelled. This meant that our income would tend to increase every month, since most members would stay with us for at least six months.

I was in Japan over the Christmas break when I got a call from my business partner, Sterling, who was manning the fort back in the United States. He was not in a good mood. He had checked the company mailbox on Christmas Eve and found that we had been sent a cancellation letter from our merchant account underwriter. We were losing our ability to process credit cards—along with all of the thousands of other Internet-based customers of this bank. They decided to cancel all of the Internet customers in one fell swoop, and to do it over the Christmas holiday. They were giving us 30-days notice of cancellation, thoughtfully sent out in the Christmas mail rush on the 14th of December.

The consequence was that we had to sit on our hands and wait until January before we could even attempt to remedy our situation. Around January 4, the banks started to open again and we tried to apply for a new merchant account with another provider. Since the bank that cancelled our account also dropped thousands of other Internet-based businesses, there was a mad dash in the new year for merchant accounts, and banks were suddenly charging $1,000 or more for an application fee because of the sheer volume of applicants surging through the system. We made the decision not to pay this kind of extortion money on principle.

January 14th came and went. Our merchant account was suspended. No new merchant account was forthcoming. It was February before banks started to talk to small businesses again. When we finally got in the door with a bank and were working through the paperwork, we provided the paperwork for our previous merchant account. This is the point in the narrative when a good storyteller would pause dramatically and say something like, "And you aren't going to believe what happened next." The new bank declined our application because of our *chargeback rate*. This is the ratio of dollars claimed as errors by customers to the total amount of charges billed. If this ratio went over 1 percent, you were considered to be in the "red zone." We were informed that we had an "infinitely high chargeback rate" of $120 (one or two customers who did not recognize the Meridian IS charge name on their statement) divided by $0 of transactions in the last month. We explained what had happened, but we were not able to secure a new account in time to keep our earned base of rebillable clients intact. The bank officers didn't care. The enforcement of this policy (without exception and without discussion) was surprisingly rigid. The business would live on, and we got payment mechanisms in place again, but the fluid transition of our accumulated rebillings portfolio was made very difficult. This cost us quite a bit of money.

Luckily, we had two revenue streams at this time, and we were able to focus our efforts on other areas (namely our data business) during this transition period.

Hope for the Best but Plan for the Worst

This is a logical strategy. Plan out what the full range of possibilities are for your business, for your project, and for your new product offering. Understand the possible outcomes, from the best possible outcome to the expected average outcome to the complete-failure outcome (e.g., not selling any product and getting sued). This exercise should be part of any project plan.

But beware: you need to make sure that in mapping out the various scenarios, your subconscious mind does not grab a hold of the worst-case scenario and nudge it toward actually happening! The trick is to be aware of some of the most likely of the worst cases, but to move past them and push forward to the best-case outcomes.

Do *not* get derailed by thinking about every possible bad thing that can happen. If you find yourself going there, just stop. Train yourself to examine only the most likely of failure points, and do not go on any fantasy excursions to the land of low-likelihood disaster scenarios. There is no point, and it will hurt more than it helps.

A great deal of our success or failure comes about because of the subtle expectations that lie just below our conscious thought. If you obsess over worst cases, you increase the likelihood of bad things happening. Do not doubt this for a second.

As for the detailed failure analysis work, have one of your subordinates do it (if you have any) and only ask for a summary of the most likely failure points.

Changing Plans Is Easier When You Change Early

Always keep in mind Seth Godin's wisdom in *The Bootstrapper's Bible* (Upstart, 1998):

> *Opportunities will try to cloud my focus, but I will not waver from my stated goal and plan—until I change it. And I know that plans were made to be changed.*

Don't resist starting over or drastically changing your approach if it is needed. If you are going to do so, however, make sure of the following:

- You carried out the best analysis you could before you got started.

- The prestart analysis used the best information available at the time, and you continued to get further information that materialized as the project (or business) moved forward.

- The further information that you gleaned from carrying out the project (or business) informed you that change (or a stop) was needed.

Avoid indecision and vacillation. If you cannot see a clear path that will take you at least a few steps forward in your business, then find someone who can help you to do so. Don't fall into the trap where you tiptoe a few steps into something and then quit, and then tiptoe into something else and quit. This fail-early rule is not an excuse for weak decision-making. It is an exhortation to decide on the best available information, keep your antennae up and receiving all available input, and be open to modification of your plans as you move forward. It is better to adjust early than to continue on a path that will not take you where you want to go.

Some businesspeople and educators are fond of the phrase, "Fail early, and often." I cannot quite grasp this. I don't like the "often" part. It indicates a pessimistic outlook by the entrepreneur on identifying real opportunities in the market, visualizing a viable path from idea to profit, and executing the plan. "Failing often" indicates a lighter commitment to the research and planning before investment of capital than I am comfortable with.

Value and Preserve Your Agility

The tension between being quick on your feet and using military-style planning (deliberate and predictable, but slow) was clearly evident after we were acquired by a larger player in the same market. My small team was able to perform miracles in productivity, demonstrating that we could execute technical changes in hours while our larger parent company would often take months. It was a matter of some pride for my tribe of bandit programmers and creatives.

The truth of the matter was that we were able to do this because we were *good* and we were *motivated* to be agile, but also because we were *smaller*. Here comes another metaphor:

Running a business is like hiking with a backpack.

When the backpack has nothing but a canteen and an extra pair of socks in it, you can freely run up and down the mountain without breaking a sweat. When you add the cumulative effects of years of business rules, customer relationships, and technical dependencies to your project, it is like loading bricks and rocks into that backpack until it is overflowing. When it comes to hiking, you will find yourself struggling to simply get out of camp—let alone show off by running up the mountainside. So what to do?

For one thing, you can evaluate whether the extra weight is worth adding on each time an opportunity to put something extra in your backpack presents itself. This means that you evaluate with a critical eye every transaction that is going to cause you a support demand. Everything that has to be tracked and accounted for as a business process is going to contribute to the weight. Every new business rule or routine added on to what your business already does needs scrutiny before you agree to it. Contracts, special arrangements for individual customers, pet projects, marketing processes, and many other things that your business will want to do fall into this category.

I suggest that you share the analogy of rocks in a backpack with your team. When you discuss new projects and responsibilities in this context, the consequences of new projects become more intuitive and context-rich. For engineers, saying, "Do we really need to add this rock to our backpack, guys?" helps them to view the project from more of a long-term perspective, where they may tend to be execution-biased (using short-term thinking) otherwise.

Keep in mind the tension between being able to change course on a dime and having to plan your moves like an aircraft carrier battle group—about 20 miles in advance. Weigh the benefit against the true long-term costs on each decision that you make, because they add up over time.

Mistakes Are Inevitable

Most entrepreneurs are *seriously* afraid of making mistakes. They often think that making a business mistake will blemish not only their businesses, but also their personal identities. This is unnecessary, and time will show that everybody makes mistakes. You make mistakes, and so do I (and everybody knows it). It is tremendously taxing to try to build up and maintain the illusion that, as the leader, you have perfect judgment and knowledge—so don't even try to do it.

Even good, robust decision-making is bound to result in mistakes. Great leaders know that making decisions quickly, getting on with it, and making mistakes from time to time is OK. The upside of this is that you get out there and respond to your environment quickly with the knowledge that there are few things that cannot be fixed. The alternative to this is slower, more paced decision-making or, worse yet, delegating all the decision-making to others—with no guarantee whatsoever that taking the additional time will make the decisions any better.

In fact, making a mistake and then owning it afterward is a great way to share your humanity with your team and build loyalty from them. Do your best at all times to get everything right, but don't paralyze yourself in the effort to nail everything on the first try every time.

Customer Complaints: Treat Them Like Gold

You can assume that for every complaint you get there are many, many more customers out there that thought the same thing, but didn't care enough to tell you about it. Consider every complaint to be the literal tip of the iceberg.

It is unfortunate if you screw up and someone is unhappy about it. But, you can (and should) strive to turn it around and make it a win for your customer and your business. If you have the chance to interact with a customer that feels wronged, find a way to fix the problem. Even if it costs you some money to do it. Don't mess around—fix the problem. Apologize for the inconvenience.

On our social networking site we would give customers free extensions of their account time—a free month, six months, even a year sometimes. It was not an out-of-pocket expense, and people loved it.

I have this exact discussion several times a year with my employees, and it is worth repeating here. A team I am managing right now is an online web brand. We touch about 5 million individual customers every month. Recently the marketing team lead was agitated and upset because a customer went to our Facebook wall and commented negatively about how hard our site is to use: "This site is completely counterintuitive! I couldn't find anything on the overview page! What are these guys thinking!" My team was upset because the user was venting, and incidentally had simply not noticed features that were right in front of him on the page.

I talked to the marketing folks as a group and reframed their understanding in the following way: "How many visitors does our site have in a month? A lot, right? If we lined them up shoulder to shoulder, how many miles would they reach?" (The marketing manager calculated at that time that they would reach 70 or 80 miles, shoulder to shoulder.) I asked them to imagine driving past them at 50 miles an hour, trying to look at each and every face swishing by one at a time. After 30 or 40 minutes you would be absolutely numb trying to see that many faces. Imagine how big that group is! Out of *all* of those people, how many are going to reach out to us and give us feedback on our site? Looking at the sheer size of that group, how many would contact us to complain if something was wrong? You might say 1 percent, or 1/2 percent … and be way wrong; 1/2 percent would be thousands of people giving us feedback—(which clearly does not happen). Of all those faces, all those customers, it is less than one in a million who take the time to contact us to say anything personal about what we are doing. The fact that they take the time to say anything (positive or negative) makes them extremely special—and worth taking the time to respond to positively. It's a miracle, don't you see? Of all the things they could have been doing in that moment, they chose to interact with you. I get a warm feeling even now, thinking about all of our disgruntled web site complainers.

The team responded to the customer, and the customer apologized for complaining—and put a positive comment on our Facebook wall. And incidentally, the customer had a valid point on improving the site, so we also learned something about how we could make our site experience better.

Takeaway: Customer feedback is often rare almost always valuable, and something that entrepreneurs often underestimate.

■ **Note**　Pause to consider before ever explicitly admitting a mistake to your customers—the noble gesture of admitting to a mistake could (in certain circumstances) find you in court with no ground to stand on if loss or damage were involved and the customer chose to use it against you.

Case Study: Adaptec

My company invested some serious cash in top-of-the-line computer gear when we were putting our data center together for Meridian. Unfortunately, the critical storage controller card for the primary database went bad right after we installed it. We were really upset, because it was supposed to be bullet proof (nothing really is bullet proof in IT, but we paid a lot to get close to perfect). We called up Adaptec, and they immediately, without questioning us, sent an overnight package with a new controller card. Not just a new card, but a *more expensive* card that was a big upgrade from the one that had failed. Wow. We went from pissed off and disappointed to fans of Adaptec. I am still happy with them, even though their product brought down part of my operations for what ended up being a little less than a couple of days.

When it comes down to it, I think that most disgruntled customers just want to be recognized as human beings and to feel that they are respected. It is not so much that they want to cause problems (although sometimes it is the case); they most often just want to be treated with respect. The inverse is also true. Always strive in every direct communication with your customers to show them your humanity. When I get on the phone with a customer, I do everything possible to establish rapport with them; this means giving them a warm greeting and self-introduction, listening more than talking, and speaking clearly and professionally. This short list is just common sense, but I have seen how bad situations can get when common sense is not used.

The Dollar Exercise

One thing that I am known for in my circles is the *dollar exercise*. I always have whiteboards in all of my work environments—one of the first things I do in my offices is cover all available wall space with whiteboards because of the importance of multimodal dialog with the team when discussing complex things. (Pictures plus notes plus words plus hand-waving equals better communication.)

In any case, when new projects, or investments of any kind of labor or capital are considered, I like to take the time to draw a dollar sign high up on the whiteboard, above any notes or diagrams. The point is then made that whatever details we draw or discuss must ultimately pass the test of connecting back to the dollar sign. If we cannot demonstrate by logic or function that the project will result (in one way or another) in value (dollars) being created for the company, then the project does not make sense, and we table it.

A number of interesting but ultimately pointless projects have been unceremoniously filed away in the "won't do" drawer because of this practice (and that's a good thing).

This chapter has given a quick look at some core business ideas that are important to me, and end up being very frequent subjects of discussion with the businesses that I mentor. The subject will now change to one that is very near and dear to me: marketing. A recurrent theme of this book is the effort required to communicate your value proposition and story to customers; I will cover a number of topics from that world in the next chapter.

Marketing

At the beginning of this book I made the following assertion:

> *Most folks think that building a product or packaging a great service is the hardest part of becoming a successful business owner. The thought is something along the lines of, "If we can just build the web site, or open the restaurant, or create the widget—then we are going to be rich!"*
>
> *Building it, opening it, or inventing it is usually the easy part. The hard part is what comes next—connecting with customers, communicating your value, and convincing them to pull out their wallets to give you money.*
>
> *Figuring out exactly how you will connect the product with enough customers in a short enough time span so that you survive, and grow to thrive—that's where the real work awaits.*

From my perspective, building technology or providing goods or services is more about marketing than anything else. In this highly competitive world, quality products *have to be a given*—there are simply too many other options for customers to choose from.

Marketing is not advertising. Advertising is just a part of a marketing plan. Marketing is your approach to interacting with the market—deciding what to build, for whom, when, and in what way, and how you will connect it with customers to make money.

Marketing is as much art as it is science. If building a piece of software is like folding an origami crane—complex and time-consuming, but following a predetermined pattern—then marketing is more like a dance where the music is constantly changing and new people are constantly appearing on the dance floor. These are two radically different processes, and require radically different competencies. The marketing dance will take many forms, and will consume a significant amount of resources if it is to fulfill its goal of connecting your product with customers. This section of the book is about that dance.

Choose Your Product Well

What comes first? The realization that you have a great idea and that you can sell it? Or the realization that you want to run a business?

It can happen either way, but in either case you have to have a proposition that will stand up to the truth of the market. A weak idea can be supported to success by excellent execution. A strong product can be a complete failure with poor execution. The best scenario is to run a company around a strong product, and then back it up with excellent execution. That combination is the stuff legends are made of.

So what does it mean to have a product that will stand up to the truth of the market?

For one thing, it means the product is *compelling*—it solves a problem for people to the extent that enough of them will reach for their wallet and give you money for it. Simple enough, huh?

It also means you can *control* it—this is called the *barrier to entry* for your competitors. Once you unleash your idea on the world, how can you protect the new niche or market that you have created? Patents and copyrights are designed to help with this. Operational excellence is another way to protect your idea. If you hit the ball out of the park, it will be harder for others to follow you.

So before you can have a business, you should have a strong product concept. Again, this can be a physical product, a service, or a combination of both. What are some of the factors that we should consider when choosing what we are going to sell, or evaluating an existing offering? Here are some starting points.

What You Have to Work With

What are your strengths and advantages? What makes you a natural fit for your industry? Every entrepreneur and every team has its unique attributes. Can you identify some unique characteristic or attribute that is available for you to leverage? You should have *some* of the following characteristics available to you:

- *Skills*: This is where most people start: their area of expertise. This should be connected with other strengths or strategy points to make the business great.

- *Experience*: Similar to skills, this is your (or your team's) history of applying skills to a task. This is the category of lessons learned, scar tissue, and wisdom.

- *Resources*: Do you have access to a unique resource that would give your business a natural advantage over your competitors? The company that acquired us is a great example of this, as they are a consortium of newspaper companies, with a tremendous set of resources within the organization (including sales staff, offices in cities across the country, business relationships, and control of television and print resources coast-to-coast). In the late 1990s, all of these resources were a great launching pad for a portfolio of online advertising brands (Cars.com, Apartments.com, HomeFinder.com, etc.).

- *Knowledge*: Distinct from skills and experience, knowledge in this sense is something that you know or have realized about your market that other companies don't seem to grasp yet (or at least they are not visibly moving on). Knowledge of a single key fact can make all the difference for a business starting up. Google realized that text-based advertising and market-driven pricing were a good idea at just the right time. That realization combined with the resources of their growing online search platform helped them create a multi-billion-dollar enterprise.

What Are You Shooting For?

The combination of attributes just mentioned can help you to identify what you should be creating as a product or service. The next step in that evaluation process is to look at how the product or service can be leveraged over time to make an amount of money for you that is worth the time and effort required. If you execute the idea well, and market forces work as you expect them to, what is the potential financial upside for your business concept in the very best case? What are you shooting for? Be very specific in what you think you can accomplish, and justify your plan to yourself by working out the numbers. In working out the numbers, you end up defining the scale at which you believe you can operate—that is to say the number and size of transactions you plan to create.

The question of scale has a couple of components: demand of the market and your capacity to obtain or produce product for sale. The market must need your product in quantity, *and* you must be able to produce enough of that quantity to meet demand.

What Is the Opening in the Market?

After identifying what resources you have to work with, look for a natural point of entry in the market itself. Consider that the marketplace is like a castle; a castle with walls and moats preventing the casual bystander, or even a fairly determined assailant, from getting inside. As with all good castle stories, your objective is to get in there, to take over a part of it. As you stand on the grassy field just below that imposing structure, you begin to study what your challenge looks like. You naturally start considering what your approach should be. Do you storm the main gate? Do you try to climb the 80-foot-high walls on the south side? What if you noticed a gap at the corner of one of the walls— wouldn't it be better to hit the gap, the opening, the weak spot where your effort for entry would be least?

Of course it would be. And marketing is no different. Look for a niche that has been overlooked or underserviced by other players in the market. Choose that as your entry point.

Once you get started, make it your objective to burrow in so deeply that you come to "own" it. Once other players notice you are gaining ground and profiting from your strategy, you are already months ahead. In many markets, this is enough protection to survive if you are committed to constant evolution— always looking for new angles. If people follow your lead and move on your niche so long as you have been adapting, morphing, and improving all along, it will hopefully be difficult for them to catch up. This strategy often forces larger players to just buy you outright instead of trying to follow you. This sequence of events worked very well with our apartment real estate site: we found a niche, burrowed into it, and then were bought by a larger competitor.

While the niche strategy is a common one, not all markets are going to have a clearly defined niche approach. Sometimes the best plan is to march up to the main gate of that castle and start battering the door down. It should go without saying that this type of approach is often best suited to well-funded and highly resourced operations.

What Separates a Hobby from a Business?

Your customers are your reason for being. If I wanted to sound snooty I would say that customers are your raison d'être—your reason for being. (Give me a moment to fetch my smoking jacket and brandy snifter.) Customers are important. If you think about it, customers and their willingness to pay you are the only things that separate your business from being a hobby. A hobby is nothing more than an activity you do that nobody pays you for. If you love fly fishing, you can promote that outdoorsy pastime from a hobby to a business just by getting people to pay you to show them how to fly fish, guide them to great trout streams, and so on.

It all comes down to the customer—to his or her willingness to listen to your message, process what it means, and then decide to fork over hard-earned cash. You have to love it when people choose to spend time with your product, and willingly pay you money for it. And in case you are wondering, no, customers are not always right. They should, however, almost always get what they want—and they should be permanently installed as the rotating, shining center of your business's solar system.

Will You Be a Whale or an Eskimo?

Eskimos traditionally depended on killing one or two whales to survive for a whole year. They risked everything on being successful in this task. Whales, on the other hand, survive by eating millions of tiny shrimp. A failure to capture any one, any thousand, or even any ten thousand of those shrimp will not matter to the whale's survival.

Businesses can operate in either mode. You can position your product so that you need only a few large clients, or so that you need to acquire many small-value clients. This is a fundamental point of analysis when deciding what business to pursue, or how to position an existing operation or product offering for future growth and stability. Neither of these options is right or wrong; each carries its good and bad points.

Early on, you are faced with a choice of which approach to take. In most cases, your expertise, product, or value proposition will dictate to you which of these choices is most appropriate. It is most common for businesses these days (especially online) to default to the mode of going for lots of relatively small transactions. It is very useful to recognize that both of these distinctions exist, and simply make a note of your choices as you set out to establish yourself in the market. The whale/Eskimo dichotomy can also present itself as your business grows, as I will describe.

For example, consider the following scenario. The fictional OJC company makes bread. They bake and ship whole-wheat loaves to several small grocery chains and have experienced 2 to 3 percent growth yearly for the last ten years. OJC gets picked up in an article on healthy eating by the *Los Angeles Times*, which is quickly followed up by a proposal from MegaMart to provide heart-healthy wheat bread for 250 warehouse stores coast-to-coast. Great deal! That is a fantastic way to grow! It is a terrific opportunity. The knowledgeable CEO knows that saying yes entails a major risk, however.

In order to meet the demand of the additional stores, OJC will have to triple its production capacity and hire extra shift workers. This entails an outsized capital outlay, which makes the CEO nervous. What would happen if they go for it and then eight months into the arrangement, MegaMart decides to pull the contract? It could put the future of OJC in question because it may not be able to cover the loan it took out to build up its factory. Left with overcapacity and a huge debt to pay, OJC could be forced to shut the operation.

The conundrum here is this: should OJC follow fast, lopsided growth? Or maybe choose slower, diversified growth? Following the diversified route, there is less risk from any one customer picking up and leaving, but lower profit potential over the short term. Our aggressive CEO may choose to take the deal, but prioritize the quick acquisition of more sales outlets to create a diversification structure that would support the company if it were to lose the large contract.

The Precious Slice

You advertise. If you *work hard* to market your product, if you spend the required time and money to put your brand and your message in front of your target audience, then something miraculous will happen: you will earn a *precious slice* of your customer's attention. It will probably be a small slice.

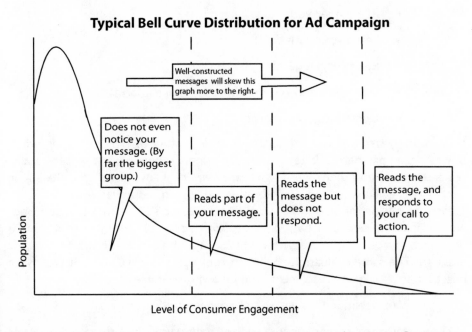

Figure 3-1. Most recipients of your message are not going to respond in any way. By creating well-formed and appropriate messages, you can increase the rightward skew of the distribution

This little moment of attention, this precious slice of thought, when combined with the right message, is what pulls people out of the zone where they don't know and don't care and eases them into the first steps of becoming your customer. (This is the hook that transitions people from left to right in Figure 3-1.) This is an opportunity. This is *the* opportunity that your business depends on. So what compact, well-formed, and compelling message will you put into that small, fleeting opening into your customer's consciousness?

The precious slice demands that your message:

- Be compact.

- Be simple.

- Be resonant to their experience.

- Have a specific intention. What do you want them to do?

  - Perform an action, such as calling you?

  - Feel an emotion?

  - Remember your name or logo?

  - Learn your name?

  - Buy your product?

  - Get interested and follow up for more information?

  - Come into your store?

In previous years, we carried out large-scale testing of our messaging when buying online pay-per-click advertising. By using a simple performance analysis, we determined that there were significant numerical advantages to including or excluding specific words in our ad copy. Adding an individual word could increase the performance of a 20-word ad by 5 percent. This means that a one-word difference between two similar-looking ads could mean over $100,000 difference in value in just a few months. Such is the power of finding the best message. The same evaluation applies to every place where you put words or images in front of your customers. The following examples are vital:

- What text and images you place in your advertising

- What calls to action you use and where you place them

- What your sales team is trained to tell customers

- What your employees in a retail store are trained to say

- How signs are constructed inside and outside of your retail location

Every possible variation of every message you put in front of a customer will have an effect. It is incumbent upon you to reach out and try to get a handle on what that effect is, and to find the most effective, informative, and value-creating message to use when you get that precious slice of your customer's attention.

More than anything, avoid saying too much or assuming your marketing targets know anything about you. The tendency I have seen is to try to impart all of the great stuff you have built into your product in one avalanche of details: "We do this and we do that and you save money and it slices, and dices, and wow—can you believe version 2.0 has the new doodlydad with print capability and ... and ... and ..."

Pick the most compelling part of your story and share a simplified, distilled version of it when you get that precious slice of customer attention. Use it as a hook to get to the next step of the conversation. Then provide more details as the customer comes in for a closer look. Your critical messaging will often be at least in part, and answer to the question asked in the next section.

Why You?

This is a question that you will need to answer. It is a question that every potential customer has in store for you, and something that you should be prepared to answer early on. A good friend of mine has been working on a micropayment platform for online commerce for the past couple of years. Early on he asked me for some input on his project, and one of the first things I asked him was rather blunt but meant to provoke thought: "Why you? Why not Google? Why not Amazon? If you want to be a platform for companies and individuals to use across the Web, how will you explain why it *needs* to be you, why it *must* be you? Why not the other really large (and well-known) players in the market?" It may be worthwhile to note that he could not convincingly answer that question, and has made a pivot or two since that time.

The "why you?" question is intimately related to the fact that most products and services can begin to fall into the parity product category if you let them. With most business models, there are multiple other options in the market that you will need to compete against to earn a customer. Take a look at pizza. How many different pizza options do you have within 10 minutes of where you are right now? Pizza is available via home delivery, Internet delivery, local restaurants, and chains such as Domino's, Pizza Hut, and Papa John's. A customer *could* even decide to head to the kitchen and make one from scratch. How many pizza brands can you find in your local store? Your grocery store probably has 30 different options for frozen pizza. Any which way you turn—pizza is everywhere.

Take a moment to think about all of the messaging you get for this one product on TV and the radio, in the newspaper and junk mail coupons, and from signs at the grocery store. All of this messaging is aimed at differentiating products from one another on some facet of the pizza experience:

- Taste

- Price

- Convenience

- Emotions (e.g., fun)

- Quality

- Local exclusivity

Just as with the pizza industry, you will have to differentiate yourself in some way to stand out, to get customers, and to grow a defensible position from which to operate.

The Internet Is Not Magic

Don't believe that the Internet is a magic solution to any business problem. It is much like any normal marketplace, but with a lower barrier to entry and potential global reach. If you look at your laptop computer, plugged into the World Wide Web, and feel electrified by the possibilities represented by that connection with so many other people, then we both have something in common. I feel it too.

Even though the Internet is a miracle of technology that has revolutionized communication and commerce, know that it is still governed by the same laws of economics that have controlled business since the earliest days of man. Remember the dot-com bubble and what were called *new economy* companies? This time saw the emergence of a large number of companies that thought that they could ignore many of the traditional laws of economics, get aboard the Internet, and ride it to wealth on the power of pure enthusiasm and limitless financing. The dream didn't last. People woke up as soon as their financing started to run dry and they realized that investors would want to see real income in order to be convinced to invest more. "No income" meant "no business," and Icarus fell to Earth with a big thump.

Traditional business (pre-Internet) was bound by distance. Limiting? Yes. But it was also *empowering*. Let me paint a picture of circumstance for you to visualize about the Internet. For our example, let's consider something traditional and cast our minds back to about the year 1750. How about looking at the business model of a cooper? (A cooper was a person who made barrels for storing materials such as gunpowder, liquids, and foods.) To survive in his local marketplace in 1750, our cooper must:

- Offer a service or product that people value. People need barrels.

- Have enough potential transactions in his local market to survive. This means a population of people within trading distance, who produce food or store liquids in such quantity that they regularly need barrels. A barrel might last anywhere between one and five years, so our cooper has to take that into account when looking for repeat customers.

- Build and maintain a good reputation. If you were known to be a cooper that once used outhouse planks to make barrels, folks might not want to buy from you.

- Find the right balance between demand and supply. For example, 40 coopers in a 40-barrel-per-year market won't work.

- Be able to source materials for making barrels. That means iron for the metal rings, wood for the barrel planks, and wood for making fires to dry the planks and heat the metal if necessary. If any of these materials are completely unavailable (e.g., in Antarctica), the cooper would be in the barrel-*importing* business, not the barrel-making business.

Because it's 1750 in this thought experiment, the cooper doesn't have access to global markets. He cannot (easily) sell his product to Paris, London, and New York at the same time. He is pre-Internet, pre-airplane, and pre–steam power. This is *local* in the most profound sense of that word.

I said that a local market is empowering a moment ago, did I not? I say that because of these two factors:

- Information is simple and available.

- Consumer options are limited.

Table 3-1 describes some of the chief differences between doing business on a local scale and a global one.

Table 3-1. Core Differences Between Local and Global Markets

Local	Global
Information is simple. In a primitive local market, you can know a significant proportion of what there is to know about the market forces at work.	*Information is complex.* In a global market, information about competition and market forces is very complex, and often hidden. Competitors and market pressures can arise from anywhere at anytime without warning.
Options are limited. If you are the only barrel maker or a member of a small population of coopers, then people need to come to you for their barrel needs.	*Options are unlimited.* For the customer that is willing to use FedEx or UPS to obtain goods, distance is not an issue. Providers from Croatia to Cleveland are going head-to-head with one another.
Relationships are strong. You meet every single customer face to face. You are not a brand—you are a person.	*Relationships are weak.* You almost never meet a customer face to face. Until you build powerful brand recognition (like Apple or Amazon), you are merely a product description and a price point.

Local	Global
Marketing is unnecessary. In a primitive local market, marketing as we know it is unnecessary. You offer a service in a town. People who need the service in the town come to you.	*Marketing is mandatory.* In a market with global reach, you can reach everybody but are known by nobody at all (at least in the beginning). It's a diabolical trade-off.
Sales volume is not volatile. You sell as much as the local community demands—no more, no less. There is relatively predictable demand over time.	*Sales volume is highly volatile.* Your sales volume is directly tied to the effectiveness of your brand positioning and marketing. The lure of the Internet is seductive indeed: "If I can reach the whole planet and everybody wants my product, then I can make a lot of money!" For the sake of making my point, I will repeat the first sentence: Your sales volume is directly tied to the effectiveness of your brand positioning and marketing.
Profit is more certain. The price that customers are willing to pay for your goods or services is likely to be at a fair equilibrium with the cost to produce your goods or services.	*Profit is much less certain.* The price that customers are willing to pay for your goods or services can vary widely from profitable to impossibly cheap. You often compete against the cheapest provider anywhere in the world.
Maximum profit is limited. The best-case scenario for revenue and profit in a local market is limited.	*Maximum profit is very high.* The best-case scenario for revenue and profit in a global market is many times higher than in a local market.

Looking at this comparison, we begin to see that *marketing is a response of business to weak relationships, distance, and customers having multiple options for a product or service.*

Takeaway: Limited distance restricts your reach, but it also means that you only have to compete with the locals. The Internet gives you access to a global audience, but also competitive exposure to any Joe with the same idea you have—worldwide.

Parity Products and the Bozo Factor

Abandon all hope ye who enter here.

—Dante

A *parity product* is something non-unique, such as books, DVDs, and software. *Indiana Jones* on DVD is a parity product—it is the same at Wal-Mart as it is at Best Buy. Parity products cannot compare to one another in terms of features (as they are identical), so the market has to search for other differentiating factors. Convenience is one. Customer service is another. In most cases the market will push and prod, and the most important differentiating factor will turn out to be price. When the differentiating factor is price, this overwhelming downward pressure continually pushes profit margins down—often to near (or below) zero profit. The game then quickly becomes which supplier can provide the parity product with the lowest-cost overhead. This is a terrible game to play, as everyone seems to lose (except the customers, who are happy that they got what they wanted—and cheap).

A complicating factor for selling online is what I have come to call the *bozo factor*. In a large enough marketplace (such as the Internet in general, and eBay.com, Amazon.com, and similar marketplaces in particular), if you have a parity product, there is never a shortage of bozos who will knowingly or unknowingly *operate at a loss* and push the prevailing lowest market price on their products below the realistic lowest profitable price. These market participants are often short-duration participants because they will put themselves out of business in short order, due to lack of profit. An example of this, and what I am thinking of in particular, are the numerous and largely anonymous participants selling products on razor-thin (or negative) profit margins on massive trading platforms like Amazon and eBay. A Darwinian die-off never really takes hold because other similar participants are always entering even as older ones go out of business and disappear from the scene. A natural selection scenario with emerging winners is only valid in localized contexts where the entry of new participants is constrained by the finite nature of the supporting population. The Internet is not a constrained or finite population, and new participants are emerging and disappearing with staggering speed and limitless replacements on their way.

In short, there is never a shortage of bozos, and the markets where they proliferate are made unprofitable for legitimate players because of the bozos' limitless loss-taking.

With parity products in large enough markets, *somebody somewhere* can always sell cheaper than you. If you are the cheapest today, then somebody else will be cheaper tomorrow. Your competitors may have advantages that make it very difficult if not impossible for you to compete against them. This is a natural (and to economists, *beautiful*) feature of the marketplace, and it's yet another reason to avoid parity product markets.

The only exception to the rule of avoiding the parity product market altogether is the highly desirable case where you can shatter the parity paradigm in some way.

An illustration of this would be if you could acquire the products *significantly cheaper* than anybody else. An example of this is buying closeout merchandise from retailers, or having an asymmetrical deal with the manufacturer that prices you differently than everyone else in the market. (This is also where counterfeiters appear on the scene. Interested in a $35 Gucci handbag anyone?)

Another way to succeed with parity products is if you can market the products to a group that has *no other options*. An example of this is the concession stand at a movie theater. You have a closed audience with no other options for purchasing a Coke or a candy bar, so you can literally charge five times the normal cost. These parity products are at their most profitable when customers have no other options.

The Two Approaches to Differentiation

No matter what your business is, your primary job in communication with your customers is to be noticed and to differentiate yourself from their other options. Moreover, you want to sufficiently separate your brand from other options so that *you* are their choice when they go looking for your category of goods or services. Another way of framing this challenge is this: you need to differentiate yourself with regard to your competitors, and to arrange your communication and strategy around these particular points.

There are two main approaches for differentiating that I have come across so far in my businesses: I call them *positional differentiation* and *structural differentiation*.

Positional Differentiation

This is the classic marketer's definition of differentiation, where you "build a better mousetrap." If you are providing a product or service, what is your story? Why is your product or service better, more convenient, better tasting, sexier, or more desirable? Every business should try to build this kind of narrative, and it must be the following:

- *Simple to explain*: Can you explain it in five words or less?

- *Believable*: Does it strike the average consumer as true?

- *Relevant*: Are the points that you make actually valuable to your target audience?

Here are some examples of businesses that use positional differentiation:[1]

- *College Painters*: This company does what many other painting companies do: painting houses. The owners know it is hard to message effectively for abstract differences like materials quality, brush technique, and so on. These guys position themselves as "exceptional college students managing their own business as interns for the summer." That is a wholesome messaging point that people respond to when choosing who to hire. "Why hire some *contractor* when you can get a great paint job for your house and also help put smart, motivated kids through college?" This is positional differentiation on the emotional resonance of a service.

---

[1] These are actual business models at work in Austin, Texas.

- *Nature Burger*: This is an un-fast-food joint that provides burgers and fries like the other guys, but does so with locally produced beef and organic potatoes. The owners make a better product, and they make sure that all of their customers know it. They actually have pictures of the ranchers that they buy from on the walls in the restaurant. When customers are making a decision about what they want to eat (and feed to their kids), they choose Nature Burger because of the environmental and health differences in the product offered. This is positional differentiation on the health attributes and emotional content of product.

- *The Joint Chiropractic*: This clinic does not accept insurance, and differentiates itself by a flat $20 fee for all services. It avoids the complications of insurance filing and copays by just charging one set fee. Most visits are walk-in and can be completed in 10 minutes or less. It appeals to busy customers because it is not too expensive, and customers can make a spur-of-the-moment decision to stop by. Less money, less hassle, less time. This is positional differentiation on cost and convenience.

Structural Differentiation

Structural differentiation is useful when your product or service is very much like the other options in the market, and/or the difficulty of communicating the unique selling points of your product (if there are any) is high. An alternative to pinning down customers one by one and explaining why you are better is to study your market and its consumer behavior to find a way to make it inevitable that you will get customers by the *structure* of your activity: where you place yourself and your messaging. Compared to positional differentiation, this is a very practical option when the market is so crowded that any complex or nuanced messaging will be impractical and ineffective. Here are some hypothetical examples of businesses using structural differentiation:

- *Joe's Pizza*: Joe makes good pizza, but he doesn't make the best pizza in the world, and he doesn't even advertise, because he bought the rights to locate his stores at several airports in his area. His business is asymmetrical compared to the competition in that he is the only choice for his target audience at a particular point in time. Customers are locked into whatever eating choices are available once they are through the airport security line and waiting for their flights. If they are at the airport and want pizza, then they are a Joe's customer. Quality, price, and other differentiators mean less in this scenario than they would in an open market (although they do help). Being the only option is a good example of structural differentiation.

- *Online Real Estate Search*: In building an online business that competes in this crowded marketplace, we implemented a visually distinct brand, but realized over time that this would not be what would make or break our success. The quality of the brand experience did not impact our reach to users (although it certainly impacted the conversion rates of users once they came to the site). Our differentiator in customer acquisition was to "always be there" when shoppers needed to find a place to live. What that meant for us was that, more often than not, when they would go to Google and type in a search, we would be an option on the results page.

We built high-quality content and executed a complex search engine–optimization and search engine–marketing strategy to satisfy that objective of "always being there." We did well because we were very frequently there on the screen when any of the 80 million apartment shoppers in the United States decided they needed to find a new place to live. Of those searchers, it came to pass that millions of them per month came to our site. This was not because of our brand position, but because of how we structured the placement and type of messages guiding them to us. Finding a way to be omnipresent as an option for the customer is a powerful example of structural differentiation.

- *MegaMart:* The MegaMart chain of warehouse stores decides to make a house brand of soda. It just puts "Mega-Mart Cola" on the label and doesn't particularly worry about trumpeting the product quality or taste. The product is then displayed prominently on the end caps of MegaMart's soda aisles. While MegaMart may choose to put some messaging behind the quality of the product, it doesn't need to differentiate product characteristics; it can use the status of *house brand* to get customers by default (so long as the product is somewhere near the quality of the alternatives). This is a case structural differentiation combined with positional differentiation: the product is simply always there, and it can be priced cheaper than the alternatives due to the higher margin.

Takeaway: You will benefit by looking for both structural and positional differentiation in your business. Take advantage of both if you can, and expect that one or the other will be dominant in what actually brings in business for you.

Know Your Customer

Knowing the market is critical. It also means knowing your competition and knowing your customer.

At one startup where I was the chief strategist, and in charge of the marketing team, I put together a tangible model of our target customer. We gathered statistics about our web site users that provided us demographics on age, ethnicity, gender, education, and so on. From this data, we determined that the single largest demographic group was Hispanic and African-American women between the ages of 24 and 32. I asked my creative team to make a life-size full-color cutout of "our customer." This female figure was then placed on a glass room divider near our break room. Several engineers reported feeling a bit jumpy while they were getting their coffee because it felt like they were being watched! We named her Valerie and surrounded her with squares of paper taped to the wall that each had an important bit of market research written on it.

So, what was the point of this? I wanted my team members to "Remember who our customer is." Each member of the team makes decisions every day that can be meaningfully informed by "Remembering who our customer is." When designing an interface for our web site: "Remember who the customer is." When deciding what kind of content we want to research and put on our web site, it's the same: "Remember who the customer is." When deciding whether to buy advertising in a baseball stadium or a women's magazine: "Remember who the customer is."

By creating an impactful visual aid, planting it in the middle of our work environment, and driving home a mantra-like repetition on the subject of knowing the customer, we created an effective tool for informing decisions made by our employees at every level of the company.

When You Have Multiple Customers

Related to this question of knowing your customer, it is common to have more than one customer to consider. When looking for an acquisition for our web real estate business, I would often refer to our task as "satisfying the three customers." We had multiple customers which could have conflicting needs in terms of how we messaged our site, spent money on advertising, and managed our business. Here are the three customers, a tangled web:

- *Shoppers*: These were folks looking for a place to live. They need information, and efficient 1-2-3 shopping.

- *Advertisers*: These were property management customers who were our advertisers. They needed to feel they were getting value for their advertising dollar. We would often find ourselves forced to make changes to the site which actually diminished the performance of the ads, but made the paying customers feel like they were getting their money's worth. This included things like writing "premium ad" above their search result listings. Shoppers click on these less, but it is easier for management customers to verify that they are getting what they paid for.

- *Acquisition partners*: These were our competitors in the market that could possibly be enticed to acquire us. This audience would be looking for a complementary brand to add to their portfolio, so we would differentiate our look, feel, and messaging aggressively even if we felt that shoppers and management customers would not respond as well. At certain periods of time, when our top priority was getting acquired, this customer's needs would win in any design or messaging debates within the team.

We needed all three of these groups, and each would rise to primary importance at different times during different periods of our growth. Recognition of these distinct customers and their individual needs was critical for us.

Image Counts

Know who your customers are and build an image that meets their needs. Who are the customers? Do you know who they are? What do they want? Why are they looking for you? Customers looking for a residential plumber are most likely going to want what everyone wants: a good service that they can rely on that does not cost too much. In this case, if your web site looks too slick, people might be scared off, thinking that your service would be too expensive. By targeting your image to the audience, you would build a site that is clean and functional and shows any industry affiliations you have.

This goes for you personally as well: always remember that image counts. That means that you may need to leave cutoff shorts and flip-flops on the floor at home waiting for your return, instead of wearing them to work. Even if you are not planning on meeting powerful contacts today, dress nicely. Get used to it. You can always tell when someone changes the way they dress for an important meeting. Their clothes don't quite fit right and they will look uncomfortable. My advice: Dress for the position you want in your industry but may not have yet.

Also, any of your staff that comes in contact with your customer is the face of the business. When they are interacting with the customer, they are *you* by proxy and they represent the company. So hold them to the same standards that you hold yourself to.

Your place of business is also up for this scrutiny. As is your business vehicles, your business cards, and the on-hold music on your phone system. Is your business e-mail at Hotmail instead of your own business domain name? All of these things should match the brand image that you have built (or are building) for your business.

Takeaway: Do an inventory of all of the things that actually touch your clients. Go through each and ask yourself if it is appropriate image-wise for the company you want to be today. Are they appropriate for the company you want to become in one year? In five years?

If You Build It, They Will Come

In the movie *Field of Dreams*, actor Kevin Costner is informed by a spiritual messenger, "If you build it, [they] will come."[2] In the story that follows, against any common sense, he proceeds to build a baseball field in the middle of nowhere—and is rewarded by throngs of visitors that congregate to take in and

---

[2] The actual quote is "If you build it, *he* will come," but using the word *they* better fits my story.

enjoy his creation. In Hollywood, this is great storytelling. In business, this is a dangerous hallucination. Unfortunately this concept carries many entrepreneurs forward and draws them into a disappointing reality when they realize that building a web site or a product is not enough. It would be awful if you put all of yourself into throwing a party, and then nobody showed up. It happens in business all the time, but it doesn't have to.

A part of any business plan should be the answer to the following question:

> *How are you going to connect with your target audience, convey the sales pitch, and convert enough of them to paying customers in a short enough time period to not only survive, but to thrive?*

Radicalize

You know your business better than anyone. You care about whether it does well. The uninformed public on the other hand does not know about your business. They don't care about it at all.

Understand that the customer coming into contact with your marketing message is unmotivated. They are very likely to be in a passive state. A passive state means that they are not moved emotionally or physically from inaction or noncaring. As I will remind you throughout this book, much of what you do as a businessperson is to fight against this passivity, against this noncaring (see Figure 3-2).

Response Distribution of People Who Notice Your Messaging

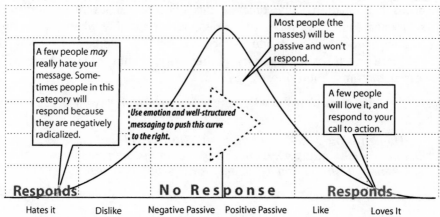

Figure 3-2. Bell curve distribution of consumer passivity to your messaging. Your job as a marketer is to push this curve to the right.

Ask yourself how you can push more people into the Love! category. Experiment with different kinds of messaging to accomplish this. At one business, we were trying to get people to talk about our brand on Twitter. My suggestion (which we did not use) was to have a contest where we put a banner at the top of our home page that said, "Twitter about us and win a water buffalo." My team laughed at the idea—nobody had ever heard of a contest like that before. The unexpected can radicalize. Our audience (Twitter users) is mainly twenty- and thirtysomethings. This generation thrives on novelty, and the online set loves to have something to share with their friends on Facebook, their blogs, and Twitter. (The fine print of this contest would have been that the winner would have a water buffalo purchased on their behalf at www.heifer.org, a charity supporting rural families in Third World. This would have cost us about $250.)

Radicalize! Emotion is the best radicalizer. Anger. Love. Fear. Hate. Use these emotions to your advantage. We found on our real estate web site that our audience (females) responded better to our calls to action if we had a picture of a baby on the page. What does a baby have to do with a real estate site? Nothing, other than that our customers clicked more and stayed longer with our brand when we had babies on the site. Emotion sells, so use it.

Never Ask Water to Climb a Ladder

Marketing staff at every company needs to compose messages that get customers to do what the company needs done. This will logically see the staff members starting a campaign or message or brochure by thinking about what they *want the customer to do*. The need is there behind what the marketer does: "We need people to buy swimming pools," "we need people to 'like' us on Facebook," "we need people to come to our web site and buy widgets." What starts as a business need then manifests itself as a piece of marketing collateral—a message in a bottle sent out into the sea of commerce, hoping for a response back.

A Marketer's Tale

The airport parking company that I use in Austin has a shuttle bus that runs from the lot to the airport terminal. I got a good chuckle out of a poster that the company had plastered on the bus windows, which said the following: "Like us on Facebook. Plus us on Google. Follow us on Twitter."

This makes sense doesn't it? Let's break it down:

- Somebody at the parking company has been tasked with the job of handling social media.

- That person's boss has probably established some sense of the metrics in the space: *likes, plusses,* and *follows*.

- Since this is what the social media person is being measured on, she creates the sign as described and posts it in the bus.

- The irony is that she has herself missed the metaphorical bus with the marketing collateral that she just made.

So what's wrong in this case? Simple: She is telling customers what her company wants them to do.

Why would any customer ever care what her company or her boss wants? Why, why, why? I would not be surprised if out of 50,000 customers per month in those busses nationwide, not a single one *ever* responds to this poster as it is written.

The Problem

Simply asking customers to do what you want is like asking water to climb a ladder. (Which just doesn't work.)

Customers are like water: Water passively courses along the path of least resistance, following its natural bias—which is to flow downhill.

A customer's natural bias is to be unaffected by most messages, only noticing and following a few of the ones that satisfy their needs in some way. The key to getting some of your customers to do what you want is to bind your call to action (like me, buy me, visit me) to a benefit that they want a part of.

What She Should Have Done

Here's what our marketer might have done differently:

1. Start with "why." Under what circumstances would customers ever *want* to interact with messaging from her brand? What do they need? What are they interested in?

2. After identifying candidate whys, then you evaluate your resources and see how you can provide a solution to one or more of them. This is the process of building a value proposition around that why. The mantra here is, "Provide value. Provide value."

3. Finally, follow up by attaching the desired actions (in this case, *like*, *plus*, and *follow*) to that value proposition.

How about these:

- "Get one free day of parking! Just 'like' us on Facebook to receive your coupon." (Value plus desired action)

- "Love Hawaii? So do we! We are sending two lucky families to Oahu—just follow us on Twitter and we will enter you to win!" (Value plus desired action)

- "A lizard in a suitcase? The funniest travel stories ever told —only on our Facebook page." (Value plus desired action)

By providing value, and arranging the message in such a way that customers who are interested in the value do what you are asking them to do, you greatly increase your chances of getting customer buy-in.

Climbing the Mountain

How do you get enough customers to survive? To thrive? The answer is that you get them one at a time. As you acquire customer after customer, you will see a pattern emerging. This pattern is universal and consists of several stages. When looking back at the life cycle of a customer who has bought your product, you can identify the stages they went through to get from "knows nothing about you" to "spending money with you" to "repeat customer, spending money with you again and again."

All of your customers are at some point completely ignorant about you. They don't even know your name. As you can see in Figure 3-3, every potential customer for your business starts here. When you open your doors as a new startup, you will begin to reach out, advertise, and communicate to your potential customers. You will advertise, and push, push, push your message out to this group, and eventually, some of your potential customers will come to know who you are—recognizing your name when they see it or hear it (a miracle!).

This is a good start, but by itself will not make you money. Your customers have to understand your value proposition before they can possibly buy anything from you. Beyond that, they have to actually believe your pitch. Pushing, enticing, dragging, and pulling your potential customers through these stages eventually yields some people that will do the unthinkable. They will actually reach deep into their pocket, pull out their wallet, and *buy*. Once you have people buying your product or service, it is your highest duty to make sure that they are so thrilled, happy, and satisfied with the experience that they will come back to you again and again. This group, the repeat customer, is the most valuable group of people in your business world.

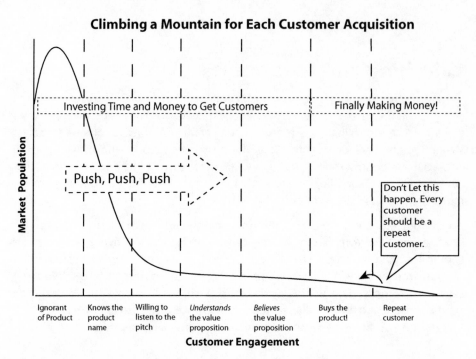

Figure 3-3. This graph represents the underlying flow of customers responding to messaging and their understanding of a business.

For some businesses, this cycle is very fast. Going back to the pizza restaurant at the airport is an example. People are hungry and don't know who you are at all until they see your sign. They know your name, see your menu, and see the pizza slices behind the counter. They know the details and feel the benefit (hungry, must eat, yum, looks good). So they buy.

Imagine how similar the same life cycle is for a car purchase. How about a home purchase? Now, how about *your* product or service? Run through the scenario of how your customers move through this pathway from ignorance to repeat customer. Look for the details; understand the gaps that might be there in the way you are trying to sell.

You must know the contours and details of this cycle inside and out. Know it, observe it, tweak it, own it. Why not put this book down right now and figure out how your different customers move through this pattern in your business? This is one of the most important exercises you will ever do to ensure the success of your business.

Learn to Love Statistics

I love statistics. They make me happy. Why? Because they give me confidence. For instance, statistics gave me confidence when I was running my first online business. Confidence was a very big deal for us because we had started where everyone starts: from zilch. When we first launched the product, we had a membership base of my partner Sterling, myself, and an account that I had made for my cat. That is a grand total of three users, one of whom was not likely to ever log in. We obviously needed to build up our list of users if we were ever going to have a real business. At that time, the big search engine was AltaVista. Banner advertisements were still "pretty neat," and had user click-through rates of over 20 percent in some cases.

OK, so I started by saying how I love stats. Here's why: we were using a service called goto.com, which was one of the pioneers in selling keyword-based click-through traffic. It was a pay-per-click model, where we would bid on a keyword phrase and pay 10 cents for every person that clicked through to our site. This is not big news now, since Google AdWords is a cornerstone of many business ventures online these days. For us, it was very important to get these bids right. 10 cents per click sounds tiny, but it adds up. We quickly got to where we were spending tens of thousands of dollars a month for traffic, and we had to get it right—if we were not capturing value, we could have gone broke in a few weeks The stats that came through this experience were beautiful to see. The aggregate behavior of thousands of visitors to our site ended up being very predictable. We could not say if any one visitor would spend money to become a member, but in aggregate, we would see that if we spent $1,000 in traffic from goto.com we would get $2,000 in sales. If we spent $10,000 dollars, we would get $20,000 in sales. This then got us into page testing to tweak up our stats.

Look for opportunities in your own business to measure return on investment (ROI) or business performance, tweak what you are doing, measure, and repeat.

Here are a couple of examples:

- For web sites, use Google Analytics, Omniture, and testing platforms like Google's Website Optimizer to create experiments where you both change aspects of your site and measure for performance. Test both major and minor tweaks—you would be surprised at how even minor and seemingly irrelevant changes can positively (or negatively) affect performance. The presence of a web radio player on one site at the top of the screen increased performance by 6 percent even though customers did not click on it.

- For service businesses, provision separate phone numbers for certain ad campaigns to measure dollars spent vs. business earned.

Never stop this process. A quote that I am famous for in my circles is

A day without testing is value forever lost.

The Marketing Mix

Every viable business has a magic formula for efficiently connecting with the right group of customers, in the right way, at a cost per customer that is sustainable. The basket of various marketing tools and methods that you use is called your marketing mix. More often than not, the difference between the companies that fail, the companies that barely make ends meet, and those that flourish, rests on finding this magic formula and executing it effectively.

Identify the best ways of reaching your audience very early on in your business. Make a list and continually adjust the ways in which you use these tools. Always be on the lookout for new ways to reach out and get your message into the right places. I remember back in the 1990s when Amazon.com was putting stickers on bananas at the grocery store. That was really out there, but here I am mentioning it to you over a decade later, so it must have been memorable.

Repeating the point: Always keep your eyes and ears open for new opportunities to reach your audience. The key to marketing is being able to discern openings in the market. This means finding and exploiting new products and services that fit in places where there are no competitors, and it means being the first to devise and press strategies for connecting your product with the people who are not *yet* your customers.

Pay particular attention to those mechanisms that you can track the performance of. Be careful not to spend too much money on mechanisms with which you cannot actually track sales. Early on, Sterling and I spent a substantial amount of money to market one of our brands with CitySearch.com. The company had an impressive office and a nice-looking sales pitch. We ended up signing a contract. We came to regret it, as there was not one sale or sales lead attributable to that investment. It hurt, because on our limited budget we did not have much money to spend on marketing, and here a big chunk went out for a year-long contract on something that was of no measurable value to the bottom line. The reason that we spent this money was that we were new to the market and we did not yet have a playbook to reach our customer. I remember feeling like it was a Hail Mary move, but we did not believe we had other options. That was neither smart nor accurate. We learned, moved on, built a playbook, and were able to grow from no customers to counting many of the *Fortune* 500 as our customers within 18 months.

There have been times in my businesses when the marketing mix was more of a single channel from which every drop of water dripped. Our relationship with goto.com was an insidious process to experience: we had a new product and needed to reach people. We were not yet getting organic traffic to our site, so we paid for traffic. There were a number of options for spending advertising dollars on the Web, but the one that was most effective was the goto.com product. What happened was a natural course of events—we pulled money from ineffective campaigns like banner ads and trade magazines and put it where we were getting good results. In the short term this was great, because we leveraged our marketing budget to get the biggest possible return. This ended up feeling like a deal with the devil because we became dependent on the traffic from that source—too dependent to be comfortable. What would happen if goto.com increased its rates? What would happen if it went out of business altogether? What would happen if it dropped us for some policy violation we weren't aware of? What if? What if? The fact is that we would have been in a tough place if something had happened to that customer stream. It did not become a terminal problem for us because we diversified our marketing and gained solid ground on the search engines, which provided a great deal of customers at a cost of $0.00. (Read zero dollars and zero cents. Free.) With multiple sources of traffic and customers, we were well diversified and had found a way to minimize at least one area of risk in our business.

In subsequent years, I have seen the same process occur again and again. The most popular mechanisms for reaching customers—eBay, Amazon.com, Google, Google AdWords, the local newspaper, trade magazines, television,

Craigslist—all of these marketing mechanisms will *try* to work well enough so that you drop all your other options and become dependent on them. This can feel easy, inevitable, and even *natural*: but it is inadvisable to succumb to the temptation to allow any one marketing source to overwhelmingly drive your value chain.

Following only optimal returns on your marketing spend can lead you to the situation you see in Figure 3-4. When you allow your business to be dependent on one marketing channel, you put yourself in a hostage situation (which is bad). What to do?

Marketing Dependency Is A Darwinian Process

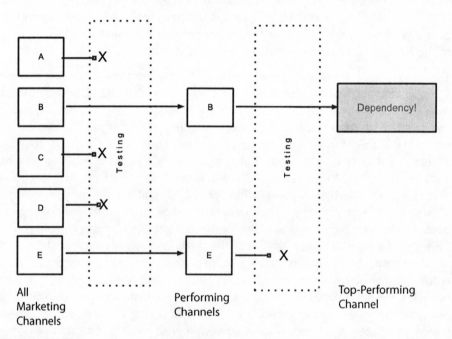

Figure 3-4. Progression from a variety of marketing sources to one winner, because it performed better than the others.

- Allow yourself to spend money on the best of the other marketing options that you are aware of that have a positive or near-break-even ROI. The options near break-even may be tweaked and made to be profitable.

- Any healthy Darwinian system has a weeding-out process, and a process of *replenishment*. Seek to replace the options that die off as quickly as possible, and initiate new marketing tests. There are always alternatives, and you must find them.

Product Pricing

Think people will buy more if you charge less? Maybe, but not always.

Case Study: Meridian World Data and Pricing

When we were building our social networking business, we needed to be able to figure out how far apart our members were from each other. When someone signed up in Singapore, they probably would be less interested in people who lived in Greenland or Australia (although you can never tell). We absolutely needed to be able to determine how far apart people lived, and what city and country they were in. The end result was that we built our own database of city and country names with latitude and longitude for each. This database had over 2.5 million entries in it before we were done and was a critical part of our business. Because we were not able to find this kind of product for sale anywhere for any price, it made a lot of sense to spin it off as a standalone business. This is an example of a choice—where you focus on one thing or chase supplemental opportunities. The decision for us was "chase on!" in this case, and we started another business in parallel by posting a simple web site called GeoData that offered a World Cities Database on CD, priced at $425.

No sales at all.

I was sure that people needed our product, but it was not selling. As a test, we bumped the price up to $1,200, and sales started coming in. Amazing! Emboldened, we created even more versions of the product at $1,200, $2,000, $3,000, and higher. The result? More and more sales. As the business grew we would eventually come to sell the product for up to $50,000. This is the same product that we could not get anybody to buy for $425.

There are four lessons that I take away from this:

- It turned out that people could not trust a product that was too cheap. They had a psychological need to spend more if they were going to trust it.

- Businesspeople spend money, and they don't want to put their reputation on the line with their bosses in order to save a few dollars of *company* money.

- It is good to offer graded versions in your pricing structure. People don't want the cheapest, and they want to feel that they did not pay for the highest either—the one with all the bells and whistles. They can settle in and feel comfortable with the one-notch-down-from-the-most-expensive product. There is substantial research to back this point up.

- The price we set was completely arbitrary. We charged what we thought we could get at first, but found by raising prices we got more sales (the first lesson mentioned previously). The fact is that by setting the *anchor point* ourselves, we were able to build a price structure that was very appealing to our customers. In a vacuum of experience (have you ever bought a data disk of cities with latitude and longitude before?), we could charge whatever we wanted within reason, so long as we were consistent. Human beings have difficulty evaluating a product or service and putting a hard-and-fast price on it, especially without points of reference such as competitors or prior experience with similar purchases.

Even parity products can vary widely in their pricing if you can convince the customer that they are not buying a parity product, but something special. Look at Louis Vuitton and Tiffany. A Vuitton handbag is a bag. It is made of stuff and holds stuff inside. There are many, many, many products on the market that do exactly the same thing. You can drive down to JCPenny and buy a bag that probably does a better job of holding stuff than any Vuitton bag and costs 1 percent of the price. *But*, my wife, for instance, would much prefer the Vuitton bag because Louis Vuitton has communicated a product message that she wants to be a part of, and the brand has name recognition.

Oprah Is Not Your Marketing Plan

Ever see a company become a big hit because it got very lucky and found itself on TV, with a tremendous amount of attention and free advertising? It is a sin of many young tech entrepreneurs that think they are going to have such a good product that people will automatically start talking about it and buzz will materialize automatically. Or worse yet, they hypothesize: "Maybe Oprah will like it!" Appearing on *Oprah* is an example of what I call the *lightning-strike* marketing model. You can get a lot of energy from a bolt of lightning, but you never know where or when it is going to strike. I don't want to be a downer, but I am here to tell you that the odds of lightning striking, and you getting a huge infusion of free marketing attention that will carry you to the promised land, are not good.

Let's look at technology: I know many programmers, as well as a lot of technology people, who are extremely good at what they do. These guys know how to *build* stuff. Oftentimes, they are also extremely naive regarding the question of how to actually connect the stuff they build with enough customers in a short enough period of time that they can survive and grow to thrive.

This reminds me of taking biology classes in college. In biology, a funny and recurrent pattern was that when the science of biology just didn't know how something works, experts would make a declaration like the one in Figure 3-5.

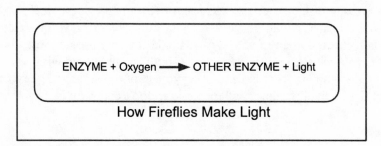

ENZYME + Oxygen ⟶ OTHER ENZYME + Light

How Fireflies Make Light

Figure 3-5. An example of an uninformative analysis of a complex process

Does this make you smarter? If you take the time to read this, you realize you don't actually know very much more about how fireflies' bioluminesce than you did before, except that oxygen and some magic is involved. Technical entrepreneurs are often similarly inclined to believe that their technology plus some kind of instant marketing miracle will make their invention into the next big thing based simply on how great their idea is (Figure 3-6).

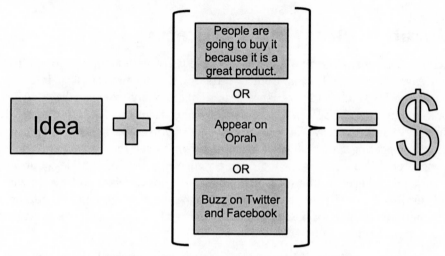

This is not a functional marketing plan.
(But smart people frequently try it anyway.)

Figure 3-6. A common, oversimplistic, and false model for describing how a business will connect product to customers

The better alternative is to plan for developing an idea and connecting it with the target population of users—one at a time if necessary. This requires money and expertise. In short, you need people that know how to market and how to sell. That is usually a different group of people than the ones that know how to actually make a piece of technology (or any product) work. This reality-based approach should serve as a *base* for promoting your product and should be reflected in all of your financial and timeline projections. On top of this base, you will then work on getting Oprah to fall in love with you or otherwise cause lightning to strike and bring you all of the fame and glory that you deserve. Chase the lightning by all means, but don't count on it.

If You Can't Measure It, You Can't Control It

The customer support group for Dell in Austin, Texas, had a huge banner hanging from the high ceiling above the heads of several hundred customer support reps. It read as the heading of this section reads: "If you can't measure it, you can't control it." Amen. What do I recommend you do with this advice? *Test everything that you can for performance. Measure everything that has the potential to feed back into your decision-making and help you to be more efficient.*

That goes double for marketing expenditures. Test performance of every dollar that you can when you advertise. For example:

- *Web pages*: Use page-tracking tools like Google Analytics to understand the performance of your web site. Use Google Webmaster Tools to set up tests to determine how to make your web site make you more money.

- *Customer surveys*: Engage customers carefully. I have found that surveys are usually answered by your fans, and ignored by the rest. You can skew your perception with surveys, but they can give you valuable feedback nonetheless.

- *Direct observation*: Hire a third party to send anonymous shoppers to your store and prepare reports on their experiences.

- *Behavior tracking*: Some grocery store chains use cameras and sophisticated tracking to observe consumer behavior in their stores—the product selection and arrangement in each store location is customized to the local demographic by using testing and feedback.

Make sure that you are aware of performance trends! Even small changes happening over time should not go unnoticed. They are the feedback you need to be able to adjust and respond to the market. You will learn the nuances of your market, such as changes in sales due to seasonality and external forces that will cause more or less sales. Knowing the cause, rhyme, and reason behind your company performance is part of your job, captain.

One thing to note with this is that I never want to spend the time to collect statistics, carry out research, or analysis on something that I know ahead of time does not have at least the *potential* to affect my decision-making. I only want to know more raw data about my business if that knowing has a likelihood of informing how I act.

Building a Team

Starting a business is a very personal thing. For me, it begins with some kind of realization or sense of need: a need to make a specific idea become real. This kernel then manifests as thoughts that bubble up again and again without conscious cause or reason. After a while, these ideas begin to gel into a plan of action, and as a series of steps that could be taken. If at some point the thoughts and planning grow to be more intense, and if the ideas pass numerous sanity and feasibility checks, then I might start thinking of concrete steps to make the idea *happen*. You will notice that at this point the nascent business is just a private internal dialog, and nothing more. Once you start acting, the first few steps are things that you can do by yourself.

But before long you will probably need to enlist the help of other people to really get it going. Beyond getting started, your business is going to need other people to understand the idea and the vision behind it. Beyond that, your business will need other people to agree to *take it on as their cause* or purpose as well. If at some point you don't have other people standing in for you as supporters of the business, then your chances of getting anywhere are very slim. In my work in startups, I have found a number of best practices and frames of reference with regard to building a team, managing it, and keeping work productive and fun. I will share some of them with you here.

Your Network Will Determine Your Success

Having a phenomenal business idea and a plan to match will not mean much without assembling a diverse network of people to help you. When I first started out in business, I did not yet understand this lesson. I had confidence in my plans, confidence in my own intelligence, confidence that I could overcome any technical hurdle that presented itself. What I did not have was the support of an experienced and diverse group of people—I was practically on my own. Looking back, I realize now that I had let fate determine my network. Specifically, my small group of friends and confidants was virtually the same a year into my first business as it was on the first day. I did have conversations with businesspeople when the opportunity arose, but I did not seek to transform that contact into any kind of relationship. Furthermore, I did not actively seek out connections that would make a difference for me. When happenstance did present a knowledgeable person to me, I did not try to establish any kind of continuing communication with them. These were mistakes of the first order—big ones.

What I did:

- Toughed it out on my own (but I learned a lot—the hard way)

- Did not join professional groups (I thought I was too busy)

- Let chance dictate whether or not I would get an opportunity to talk to helpful people again once I met them (plain stupid)

- Believed that there were not any resources available to me, even if I were to seek them out (false)

- Believed that people would not really be interested in helping me, even if I were to ask them (false)

What I should have done:

- Sought out qualified people as friends and associates that could advise me

- Joined professional groups

- Kept in touch with incidental contacts that were good sources of advice

At that time there was no Internet—so *social networking* was not even a known term. It was offline, analog, and old school. With technology being what it is today, there is no excuse for that kind of isolationist approach to anything.

Don't work in a vacuum. You need to mix and network with people. You must

- Know customers.

- Know competitors.

- Know industry folks.

- Know unrelated folks—look for synergies.

- Use LinkedIn, Twitter, Quora, Facebook, and other online networking mechanisms.

- Attend industry events.

- Speak at events.

- Build your *personal brand* and establish yourself as a hub in your business or subject matter community.

The Best Employees Would Do the Work Even Without the Job

My current venture has been particularly good with regard to employees. In some sense, we have grown a dream team of individuals who work well together and whose output is imbued with tremendous quality. The way I put it is that most of my team members are doing for the company what they would be doing on their own, even if they weren't being paid for it. We have a great arrangement where they do what they love (for the company) and get a salary.

They are motivated to do well, and they enjoy themselves. They even get paid for it. Everybody wins, and I fiercely protect the psychological environment that allows this to take place.

I encourage you to look for this kind of employee. The signs are clear. Look for people that are already doing their skill as a career, and, in their job interview, find out what they do in their spare time. I am always very interested in finding employees that *live* what they do in and out of the office. For example, the best programmers are the ones that are at home on the weekends doing what they do as their office job. For instance, tweaking server configurations in their living rooms, or performance-testing data structures. When I hear things like, "I was benchmarking a queue system on my Linux cluster at home this weekend," I know that this is the right kind of person to be doing queue systems for the business during the week. No doubt. In cases like this, what you have is an employee who *is* something, not a just a person who *does* a something. It is a subtle difference, but very profound.

The Psychological Contract

Motivation and enthusiasm from each individual in a company is important. Your employees need to feel the importance of success for the company from within themselves, not simply be held in check with company policy and performance guidelines. This can only happen if you have nurtured the *psychological contract* between you (your company) and them. This is a long process that permeates every single interaction that occurs between employee and company.

The psychological contract is the basis from which an employee will decide

- How much quality to put into the job

- How much loyalty to put into the company

- How much energy to contribute to the team

- How much off-hours time to devote to thinking about your company's success

- How much care with which to handle your customers

Does this sound important yet? It should.

So, how do you build a robust and healthy psychological contract with your team? You have heard this since you were a kid: follow the Golden Rule. Treat your employees as you would like to be treated if you were in their shoes. Respect, honesty, and appreciation for effort will get you started.

The subject of the psychological contract in itself could fill up a very long book. Short of making a book out of it, I have compiled it into a list, or more specifically a kind of informal contract. This contract is something that each of my employees gets a copy of when we do performance reviews. This agreement sets a contrast to the usual tone of a review, which is, "What have you done?" and "What will you do for the company?" This is all about how the manager works to fulfill the needs of the employee, which is the cornerstone of any manager relationship in my opinion. This is particularly applicable to knowledge workers and creative workers. In the form presented here, it is less applicable to hourly workers who do things such as man a cash register or work in a call center. This contract is custom-tailored to knowledge workers in many of its details, as most of the people who work for me are engineers or creative professionals.

A Contract for Your Team Members

So much of the discussion between employees and employers is about what the employee needs to do for the company. This is a necessary and valuable topic, but I have found it useful to turn the discussion around by giving the people that work for me a commitment on how I will help *them* to be successful. Here is the contract I offer team members:

My Commitment

1. **To provide you with clear instructions and clearly define what is expected of you.**

2. **To make sure you have the resources you need to be successful.**

   This includes

   - Time
   - Information

- Equipment
- Budget
- Cooperation from other team members

3. **To protect your interests.**

   This means

   - To always try to protect your time. I don't want you to spin your wheels on projects that won't make a difference to you and to the company.

   - To always try to protect your career. While this does not mean that things will always work out, if I am part of the conversation, you are being watched after to the best of my power and ability.

4. **To help you to grow and reach your goals.**

   This means:

   - To strive to get you the training you need to enhance your skill set.

   - To give you the opportunity to make mistakes and to learn by doing.

   - To actively seek to help you grow your responsibility to include new areas as your knowledge and skill improves.

   - To give you advice and encouragement designed to nudge you toward your best potential, even if that means you eventually grow beyond the company.

5. **To make sure your contribution is visible to others.**

   This means

   - Employees should get credit for everything they do. As your manager, I will make sure this happens. I know that nothing demotivates quite so powerfully as a manager smiling his way through the process of taking credit for what his subordinates created.

6. **To not micromanage. You own what you do.**

This means

- I recognize that the best employees *own* what they do. Their work should be an expression of themselves. If a manager gives too much direction or restriction, then it strips employees of the opportunity to express themselves and invest the full power of their creative energies.

A fellow entrepreneur recently shared a story about Sam Walton from early in his career. He was a founding member of the Procter & Gamble/Wal-Mart customer team in northwest Arkansas. This assignment gave him the opportunity to observe Sam Walton in person. He was deeply impressed with how Sam would start his meetings by asking what his senior managers had done for the employees in the last week. He would say that if they were not making support of employees "job number-one," then they could go work somewhere else. I think I would have liked Sam.

Manage Different People In Different Ways

Of all the employees I have had the opportunity to work with, every single one of them was a unique expression of personality, talents, weaknesses, needs, attitude, and enthusiasm. In other words, we are all human beings. Big news, right? Ask yourself if you take this into account when you manage your employees. If indeed every employee is unique, then the way that you deal with each employee should ideally be unique as well (I am contemplating the relationship between you and the employees that report directly to you). A one-size-fits-all mentality fails to capture the nuance needed for a real and dynamic team. Some people need more instruction, some less. Some prefer written communication, some verbal. Some people are visual and benefit from working on a whiteboard, some not. If you treat all employees the same, then I would suggest to you that you are missing something.

Learn how the individuals on your team think and how they prefer to work. (Note that this doesn't mean that company policies apply differently to different individuals.) For instance, on my team now there are employees that need top-level objectives only, and know so much about our business that they can be left to fill in the blanks on the details. There are some employees that need close management of details. And some employees have less experience and need a mentoring role to support them.

Accommodate them with a management style that fits them and they will perform significantly better. I have found that this accommodation on the behalf of the manager can mean the difference between disgruntled and unmotivated employees on one hand, and motivated, engaged, and productive employees on the other.

Employees are the backbone of your business, and believe it or not, less squeezing and more helping from management will increase performance.

Friends as Employees

At age 23, I started my first company. As any business owner does, I always needed reliable people to help me on projects. I did not yet have a deep network of business relationships and subcontracting companies, so I would do what seemed natural—I would recruit people that I knew. In one memorable case, I hired a high-school friend to work for me. I remember that he was really excited about it. The problem was that he would show up at the job site when he wanted to—he was treating our *work* relationship as a *friend* relationship. Fact is, he impacted my schedule and cost me money because he was unreliable. On finishing our first job together he remarked to me, "That was fun. We gonna do it again?" I replied honestly, immediately, and directly: "You were consistently late and didn't even show up on the second day of the project because you were hung over. What was all that about?"

Sadly, that was the last time he and I ever spoke. Really, I should not have hired this friend to work in a professional capacity with me. Looking back, his personality was not well suited to it.

Other personal relationships have yielded similar problems, all stemming from this point: when friendship—which means that people have equal status with one another—blurs into a boss/employee relationship (where what you say is what they have to do), it can cause conflict. In almost all cases, the interpersonal boss/employee position of "my way or the highway" and the buddy position of "we are friends of equal status" have great difficulty reconciling with one another. If an employee makes a mistake, you have to point it out. If they perform poorly or have a bad attitude, you have to hold them accountable. With friends, these situations are problematic and often lead to an end or permanent change (for the worse) in the relationship.

I think I should share something with you. This next story should likely remain buried, but this is nothing if not an archaeological expedition. Way back, I offered to make a teacher of mine an employee/partner in my Horizon Services business. That is, I would treat him as a revenue partner but he would just help on executing jobs and would play no part in all of the background effort of running the company. It was a very generous offer on my part, if I do say so myself. It quickly became a completely regrettable situation. As it was, he was a good friend of mine who needed some money. I looked up to him, so I thought it would be a great benefit to have his drive and intelligence helping me out. It wasn't. It was awful. He would not want to work on certain days. He would expect half the money cleared from each job, even though I had a lot of expenses I had to cover that he would never see, such as equipment payments and advertising. He actually made more money than I did! What would really make me annoyed was when I would drop by his place to pick him up at an appointed time, and he was not ready to go. He would invariably be casually eating cereal in his kitchen, not even dressed yet. Every time I think about this situation, even years later, my blood pressure starts to go up.

Now you are no doubt thinking, "*Fire* him already!" and you are right. The problem was that I had an important relationship with him outside of work, which I would damage or throw away if I were to lay it on the line and tell him to get stuffed. I was sorely tempted on several occasions to do just that.

It came to that anyway, and for good reason. But for the few months that I tried desperately to make both the work reality and the personal reality play nicely with each other, it was pure hell. What a mistake!

For the sake of completeness, I have to throw this in. On the start day of what was the biggest contract I had ever landed, he arbitrarily decided, as the not-on-the-hook-for-anything partner, that he was not going to work. To this day, I don't know what he was thinking, but he refused to get moving and insisted that I do the same. Like an idiot (remember, I was very young), I caved in and we delayed start on the project.

The customer fired us (well, me, actually) and demanded that his huge deposit be returned immediately. That was such a painful lesson. Looking back on it I am ashamed, embarrassed, and regretful. I don't have many such memories, but this one was an unmitigated disaster. Everything about sharing my prosperity with this (once) respected friend was a complete and utter failure. I am feeling sick as I write this. I fired him as a partner, and soon thereafter as a teacher and friend. The upside of all this is that I learned the following lesson that I can share with you.

Takeaways: Keep your personal and business relationships separate unless you can follow these guidelines:

- Lay all expectations out beforehand: start time, finish time, the responsibilities, who makes decisions, and who is paying for what. Discuss everything in a frank and direct way. Don't pull punches—*say* what you need to say before you get started. For example:

    - I need you here at 8:00 a.m. sharp every day.

    - If you're working with me, I will treat you like any other employee—and you will treat me as a boss. I'm serious about this, and if that makes you uncomfortable, this arrangement won't work, and the job offer is off the table.

- Hold them accountable.

Friends as Partners

As you know, it is very common for friends to come together as partners to do business. This is especially good when you are starting from scratch and everybody contributes in defined ways to build something together. Some of the most productive work relationships I have had are of this type. It has always been so much more powerful to move from friendship to partners building together than from friendship to employee.

The advantages of friends as partners are

- They know you.

- You know them.

- You have a framework of trust. This framework exists between the two of you, but also extends to your shared network of friends and family. This web of relationships adds substantial strength to a business partnership that supports you and provides arbiters and perspective-givers when the going gets tough.

The disadvantages are

- Network diversity can be impacted. When I partnered with Sterling to found Meridian Internet Services, we were a great fit. One thing we recognized at the time, however, was that we both knew the same group of people. We found that since our networks overlapped so much, we did not have the benefit of networking that would have come from relationships with diverse and separate groups of friends.

- Friends tend to be similar to one another. The dynamism that can come from having a business partner that has a different background, a different temperament, and a different attitude from you is often lost in friend-based partnerships.

- Legal formalism is reduced. You may feel comfortable doing things without contracts—since you are friends. This can come back to bite you. It has worked out OK for me, but it would have been preferable to have known exactly where my partnership stood with regard to a number of issues over the years. The informal status was easy, but uncomfortably ambiguous much of the time.

On balance, having friends as partners is a desirable situation. The basis for my personal evaluation of what would make a good business is anchored in the question, "Who around me can share my enthusiasm in such a way that they can contribute instead of just being along for the ride?" If the answer is there in the form of someone you already know and respect, then run with it.

If you are forming a partnership, sign a contract up front. I know that this can seem overdone and formal for friends or family, but it is for the best. The contract lays it all out there. If you don't have a lawyer, as a last resort, you can find a boilerplate contract document online and modify it to fit your needs. Be forewarned that this kind of contract can be very difficult to get right, but the benefits for having the understanding down on paper cannot be underestimated.

Hire Well or Not at All

Back in about 2002, my company Meridian World Data enjoyed a surge in interest in its product, and my partner Sterling and I felt we had an opportunity to greatly expand our business. We got a new office, new furniture, a phone system, and servers, and we were ready to take on the world. The concept of Meridian World Data was solid. We had customers and a growing list of people who were lining up to buy our products. We "owned" a significant number of important keywords for our industry on the search engines and we were the only player of our type in our market. As a small operation, we were very excited to have nearly $1 million of new sales leads written in a list on a big whiteboard in the middle of our office.

It was with this sense of optimism that we set about hiring a group of salespeople to expand our capacity to make profit and reach new heights. The fact is that Sterling and I were both pretty tired of having to do everything for ourselves.

As background, Sterling and I had great success with making phone calls to potential clients and getting sales. With our knowledge and sense of ownership of the product, we had a very good closing rate from phone call to purchase of product. Our commercial licenses averaged about $2,000, but they went as high as $50,000, so there was a good incentive to close as many leads as possible. But it was time-consuming and we wanted to hand the process over to a dedicated sales staff. With the recent office expansion, we did not have a lot of extra cash to commit to high salaries for our new sales team. It was decided to heavily weight salaries toward commission. We brought two people in and gave them around a $35,000-per-year base, plus commissions. We also handed them tasks relating to product enhancement, general office work, and sales.

To cut a short story even shorter, the result was that we had two salespeople sitting in an office only half trying to hide the fact that they were looking at porn sites instead of working, who made zero dollars in sales over several depressing months and successfully burned up our whole list of potential clients by making repeated inept and ineffective contacts with them.

Ouch.

So then, what did I learn with this exercise? Well, for one thing, if you are going to delegate something as important as contacting potential clients, you had better make sure that the people you're delegating to have the training and experience required, along with the right attitude to treat your customers (the most important of all resources) with the respect and careful handling that they deserve. In point of fact, we probably should not have handed sales to people who weren't owners at this early stage.

The old adage is usually true: you get what you pay for. We tried to hire people on a budget. What we thought we could afford was $15 to $20 an hour, plus a generous commission structure. We would have actually made a lot more money if we had paid a single highly qualified salesperson $40 an hour with a smaller commission structure. The problem for us was that we needed to make sure that we could pay the bills as they came in, and we only knew we could do that if we had sales to go along with the new employees—thus commission-heavy compensation. In the end, it may have been the case that we were not yet ready to hire multiple additional employees. Clearly, hiring just one individual with a better attitude and some good sales experience would have been the better thing to do.

Hiring the wrong person can really hurt, as we found out, especially when you are just starting your business. Consider hiring new folks as contractors for 90 days before committing to them as full-time employees.

Lead by Example

As the leader, a policy of "do as I say, not as I do" just won't cut it. Always, always lead by example. If you want attention to detail from your team, then you need to pay attention to detail. If you want creative thought, then think creatively. The difference between what a regular employee brings to the business and what you bring is called *ownership mentality*. Ownership mentality is the driving force behind fixing and avoiding problems, gaining new business, and promoting excellence in a business. It is the force of caring about the result, not just caring about getting to Friday at 5:00 p.m. It is the state of mind that *takes it personally* when you lose an account or have a bug in your software. Ownership mentality cannot be taught directly—that would be like telling somebody how to feel (kids, you are required to love broccoli!). This does not work. It can be caught, however, when it is demonstrated over time, and when employees are allowed to express themselves adequately and own what they do.

As a young entrepreneur in the construction industry, one of the things I realized early on was that when my team of workers would start to drag their butts near the end of a long day that was my cue to jump in and double my own efforts. I remember fondly the looks on my employees' faces when my 160-pound self would take over the work of one of the 250-pound heavyweights that had run out of steam. The look of surprise was precious. The result was that they would all pick up the pace, not wanting to be outdone. No one likes to be outdone—and enthusiasm is contagious.

Motivated Employees Are the Key

The best employees are those that care about your business. One employee that really cares about whether your business survives, thrives, or dies is worth more to you than a room full of unmotivated ones that are just showing up for a paycheck. Motivated employees are exactly what you need to progress from a company that is just *you* to a self-regulating company that can stand on its own, and eventually into a self-determining company that will fully function without your input. This progression, as discussed elsewhere in this book, is of critical importance to you if you are eventually going to want to release your company by sale or delegation into other people's hands. If you can confidently tell me that you want to spend the rest of your life managing the same company, then please ignore this chapter and skip ahead to the next one. Motivated employees are the key.

If this is so, then how do you get motivated employees? First off, this kind of employee is not simply found; he or she is often *grown*. You will probably never get somebody off of the street that suddenly and inexplicably decides that they love your company and identifies with you and your mission from the start, unless you are a brand like Google. Getting a team that cares about your business is a process, which takes time.

Employees will not viscerally care about your business unless they can see their contribution to it as a matter of identity. If an employee cannot do her job and then point at the result and say, "That was me," then it will be very hard to grow her to a point where she cares deeply about your joint success. The exception to this is when you are a well-known brand such as Disney, Coke, or Google. You can hire employees to repaint the broom closet who may end up taking pride and ownership in their contribution just on the merits of your famous name. As a small startup company, you will have to earn employee buy-in the hard way.

Find a way to engage your employees. Revenue share is one way. Having an articulate, understandable, and concrete story that describes the purpose and meaning of your business is another way. Giving employees responsibility to make decisions and shape outcomes is another way.

The best answer to this question of growing great employees will be subtly different for every business. Look at your particular business model and see what fits for you. The key takeaway is that acquiring engaged employees should be one of your primary goals. Look, learn, and challenge your team—don't settle for people that are just showing up for a paycheck.

Your Extended Team

Beyond the employees that you hire, there is a cadre of additional team members that every business will need to find, and establish relationships with. This group includes lawyers and financial folks for sure, and will likely include external vendors, suppliers, and contractors as well.

It is tempting to treat these relationships in a purely transactional way—that is, to think, "We pay 'em, and they work." That is true, but for the most important of these relationships it is not good enough. The smart entrepreneur will make it a point to humanize these relationships and create personal bonds with these critical outside players. These vendors and professionals will be critically important from time to time, but you are sharing them with many other people. Having a first name–basis relationship with them, sending them an occasional gift when they do a good job for you, interacting with them on Facebook, and otherwise treating them as friends can go a long way toward making sure that they treat you right, and will be there for you when you need them.

Have a Good Lawyer and Put Him on Speed Dial

In case you haven't noticed, the world we live in is governed by neither good-will nor common sense. Both of these admirable traits are abundant around us (most of the time) when we are dealing with individuals, but are often missing entirely when individuals give way to companies, corporations, and the laws of the land. Because of this, make sure you have a good attorney, and consult with him or her frequently.

The first lawyer I had for an early company of mine was, well, how can I best describe him? Well, the best thing I can say is that he was a nasty piece of work. After getting to know him, he was soon sharing schemes with us where he would not pay his credit card bills, but would buy the debt for pennies through some kind of back door. He took a kind of sinister pride in warping the law for his own benefit. Our relationship ended before it really got started because it quickly became clear that he embodied one of the ugliest sides of the legal profession—the application of rules without morality. We moved on and met a competent and upstanding attorney who I continue to work with even years later.

The benefits of having the close association of legal counsel are many:

- Common sense is no substitute for knowing the law.
  There are legal precedents and reasons beyond your understanding for every detail and nuance in a contract.
  Don't even begin to think that you can deal with this kind
  of thing on your own. The consequences of specific word
  choices and the presence or absence of certain clauses in
  any contract will often only be revealed in court if it
  comes to that in the worst-case scenario—and that is not
  the time to find out that you were not adequately
  protected.

- Without an attorney, you are more likely to simply accept any contract you are presented with. With an attorney reviewing every contract, you are more likely to negotiate, and to effectively shape your agreements in a way that supports your long-term best interests.

- You will be more effective in responding to threats made to you. If you become successful and get noticed in business, people will come after you and try to sue you. It is an unfortunate fact of life. Competent legal staff is a must and will often be able to help you stop such actions as they start, instead of allowing them to fester and become full-blown problems that could threaten your business.

Here is one anecdote that I like from early in my Meridian Internet Services days. We were a very small company and unable to get out of a bad service contract that we had signed with an Internet facilities company in Austin. After a year or so we found that we were locked into a package of expensive services that was billed at far over the market rate. The company refused to negotiate with us on bringing the price down to a reasonable level. There had been some service outages during our relationship with the company, so we used this to our advantage. We just had our lawyer put a short letter on his letterhead describing the impact of the service outages. We were out of that relationship within the week. That is a simple example of how even a faint whiff of legal intervention can help you to bring reasonable behavior back to a business relationship.

Lawyers: One Size Fits All?

As a new entrepreneur, I did not realize that having a general attorney is not enough to solve many of the specific scenarios I would face. You too will eventually need specialists. Would you go to a family doctor for laser eye surgery? No, you would find an ophthalmologist who specializes in laser surgery to fix your baby blues. The same applies to attorneys. When the chips are down, it is critical that your attorney be a specialist in solving the kind of problem at hand. One unfortunate tendency is that there is a financial incentive for your general attorney to offer to help you with things that are outside of his or her specialization. And if you don't know any better, what could be easier than to ask them to do whatever you need? This happened to some of my entrepreneur friends some years back, as they were represented in court by a friendly and willing contract attorney who had absolutely no courtroom experience. After a painful 18-month court case, they lost.

There are many types of attorneys: contracts, real estate, civil or litigation, mergers and acquisitions, environmental, and so forth. Don't ask your attorney to represent you in anything that is outside of his or her experience and comfort zone. As an attorney friend of mine recently noted, there is an every-changing body of knowledge in each area of legal specialization, with court precedents being set and changing laws at the local, state, and federal levels. He sharply noted that there is way too much to know in any one area for an attorney to effectively cover more than one base for you. You need a general counsel to be there for the day-to-day transactions and questions, but make sure that you and he understand when it is time to call in specific help. Don't let him even try to cover everything all the time.

Getting the Most from Your CPA

Until you are big enough to have full-time financial folks managing your accounts, you are likely to end up hiring outside companies or individuals by contract to help you to keep everything in order. Especially when it comes to handling your taxes, a CPA or accounting firm is really important.

My experience is that these professionals are not going to understand the nuance of what you are doing with your business financially, and will not come near to fully grasping your story—even if you document everything and spell it out for them. These individuals are not close enough to the decisions that you make every day, and have made in past years, to really get everything, unless you press the point and follow up on every detail. A CPA falling off the turnip truck and missing a few details can have tremendous consequences for you—and none of them good.

A CPA that I know provided the following insight into the mindset that comes with a client relationship when handling the books: CPAs will take the path of least resistance, which means erring on the side of safety (and thus higher tax) if they do not explicitly understand any particular detail of your financial story. This means they are primarily interested in avoiding regulatory mistakes, and much less interested in making sure that you get every penny that you could reasonably claim.

This has happened in my businesses repeatedly and has been a drain on finances and time. So what to do?

- Because you are going to have to push your financial folks on certain details, this means that you have to know something about tax law and financial law. You cannot farm out everything to your CPA. Find out about recent changes to tax law and the best strategies to navigate it.

- Prepare your documents carefully.

- Make a checklist of your assumptions and ask for an initial by each point from your CPA.

- Ask questions frequently—I have always ended up saving a lot of money in taxes when I stopped to question my CPA's assumptions.

- After you have asked, if you have any lingering concerns, ask again. If they don't like your attention to detail (many won't), then find another firm to represent you.

Vendors

Another important group of team members comes in the form of the various vendors and service providers that you will develop relationships with over time. I have found that vendor relationships tend to evolve to into highly valuable (even critical) symbiotic relationships over time. Such types of relationships include those with wholesale distributors, advertising partners, and software and equipment providers.

My advice for this type of relationship is to treat your vendor partners (the people) in a very considerate manner. Treat them with respect, share information with them, and stay on good terms with them even when times are tough. Appropriately, as I write this section of text, I am sitting on the patio of the Sand Hill Resort in Silicon Valley, having just participated in a Google-sponsored networking event. I am here because of the relationship with a vendor (my Google sales rep), and the fact that we just worked through a tough licensing discussion a couple of months ago.

Some years ago, during a period when I was involved in online retail, we developed relationships with our wholesale vendor reps that were critical to our operations. Through strong relationships with the vendors (the *people*, if not the companies in question), we were able to get increased discounts, extended credit, and even information on the buying patterns of competitors. This was a feature of our personal relationships with our reps. We would even send baskets of chocolate and baked goods to them during the holidays. I remember us discussing how that was always the best $80 we could spend.

Other businesses I have been involved with have gotten early access to new products, marketing exposure, special assistance, advice, and even intercession with unrelated issues where our vendor reps had connections. Vendors are potentially very valuable allies—and they should be because they need your business. Don't let the fact that you send them money or have options with other competitors find you complacent or dismissive of these folks. Keep your options open, honestly communicate if you have issues or problems, and negotiate hard on price, but keep the human relationship well maintained. It is good karma, it's the right thing to do, *and* it has the potential to benefit you and your company in ways you may not expect.

Communication Matters

What is the purpose of communication? In business, the desired outcome of communication is to get work done (internal) or to generate revenue (external).

I have a great interest in communication as it pertains to business. A few years ago I conducted a research project on communication in international projects that included nearly 100 engineers and managers from over a dozen companies. The underlying thesis of this study was my belief that *communication is the most critical component for effective management of teams.*

If you are an experienced manager, or simply have a good imagination, this should not come to you as a surprise. Of course, communication is vital—it is the glue that brings individuals together into a team. Whether it is communicating a value proposition with customers, a strategy to management, or details of a plan to a team, communication is one linchpin that you must get right. No two ways about it.

Repetition

When communicating an important message to your team or to your customers, it often pays to first decide what the important core of your message is, and then plan ahead of time for ways to repeat that core message again and again to your audience.

When communicating with your customers, plan to tell them the message and repeat it. Repeat. Repeat. Pick the most valuable message and focus on it. Have salespeople tell the customer, have your web site tell your customer, and have printed materials tell your customer the same message. Phone touches should repeat the message. Pick your most important message and repeat it until the customers get it. It may take ten messages before they get it. Keep at it.

Training and management are the same way. Managing thought and understanding in teams will find you needing to repeat and reaffirm those things that are important in your organization again and again.

Here are some examples:

- In an engineering project, I verbally repeat the objectives every time we meet. The team has heard the objectives 25 times by now, and we are just getting started.

- For marketing, there are mantra-like objectives that the team has heard from me repeatedly, such as "provide value" and "don't bury the lead."

- For management, the repeated patterns include "What is the specific intention?" and "How will we make money with this?"

It is not enough to simply tell somebody something. If it is important, repeat it until they get it. (Even once they have gotten it, it is still advisable to repeat it as long as it continues to be important, just to make sure.)

Multiple Layers

In doing research on how effective international engineering teams work together to produce highly complicated products, one of the most important lessons I learned was the idea of using multiple layers for communicating. That is to say that if you're going to focus on important details in a meeting, you should follow up afterward with another layer of communication that reinforces the same message. Usually this would be in an e-mail or a printed handout that lists and summarizes the most important takeaways from the meeting. For the most complicated subjects, the meeting should also be preceded with the distribution of materials outlining what is scheduled to be discussed in the meeting, so people can prepare a mental context and do research if required beforehand.

The concept of providing multiple layers and chances for an interested (or even disinterested) audience to get the message you are trying to communicate applies both in and out of the office. Let me explain: when putting together a marketing campaign, it is very common to provide multiple layers of the same message. For instance, a sales e-mail might be followed up with a phone call and a request for a potential customer to see a web site that has PDF documents and video on it. By providing multiple types of information, you increase your chance of communicating successfully with interested parties—those people that really want to know what you are talking about. You also increase the chance of getting at least some of your message through to people that originally did not want to know what it is that you are trying to communicate. If you provide multiple types of messaging, you will find that some customers are predisposed to prefer one type of message over another, and your chances of getting through increase when you provide multiple layers of communication. An example of this multimodal communication is as follows: start by sending an e-mail (text) that includes a link to a video (visual plus sound), followed by a phone call (verbal) and then printed materials (text plus graphics).

Never Assume

In business you should never assume anything.

If you are not sure, then find out how to become sure. Get in the habit of double-checking your facts. If I hear anyone on my team say "I assume . . ." I ask them politely but firmly to delve into the matter with a purpose and find out the *definitive answer* to the assumption, and promote it to a known and verified fact.

I have repeated this sentiment to my team so many times that, mercifully, I don't have to say it any more. If someone utters an assumption, I can just give them the look—you know, where the eyebrows go up a bit and the eyes seem to say "really?" They immediately recognize that what they have to do—go and make sure.

"I Don't Know" Is a Powerful Statement

If you don't know, just say so. It is not a sign of weakness. On the contrary, for a competent team member to say "I don't know," it is a sign of confidence from my perspective.

Don't waste time by lying to yourself or others if you don't have an answer. If you don't know, say so and then go find somebody that does—and learn.

Communications Case Study: Valerie

Way back in the 1990s, we were operating a social networking business, and in time we had nearly 1 million users and a staff of less than 10 people. We learned the hard way that customer support is a serious responsibility. What started out as a few letters sent by e-mail to our inboxes became a torrent of requests and required more than a full-time job to handle it all. And in less than a year from opening for business. As we built up our user base, we naturally needed to help people with technical problems, refunds, photo uploads not working, forgotten passwords, and the like. There was a problem though: people would get pissed off. Frequently. The accompanying screenshot gives an example of the type of communication we would receive from customers.

> Customer: "My account doesn't work. Help."
>
> Support: "Please let me know your user name, and describe your problem so I can help you. -Darrin@customer_support"
>
> Customer: "You guys can go get stuffed for all I care. Give me a refund or i'm calling my lawyer."

Ouch. It was an interesting window into human psychology, and a real wake-up call for my staff to have to deal with this kind of problem. And it was happening all the time. What to do?

We used a fancy strategic nugget that fixed the problem immediately. It was simple, cost nothing to implement, made us smile to ourselves, and made the customers respond in a more constructive manner. All of which saved us untold thousands of dollars. Drum roll please ...

> Customer: "My account doesn't work. Help."
>
> Support: "Please let me know your user name, and describe your problem so I can help you. -Valerie@customer support"
>
> Customer: "Oh, it is 'shamrock_77, and it looks like my credit card did not go through right."
>
> Support (As 'Valerie'): "It looks like it just went through this afternoon, so you should be all set! :) "
>
> Customer: "Thanks so much, you guys are great!"

Do you see the difference here in the text? This may seem like a joke, but honest to Pete, people (both men and women) always responded nicely when our e-mail persona was "Valerie." It was still the same customer support folks—usually single, geeky men trying to get through a mountain of requests—but when we metamorphosed them all into our perky customer support princess, the sailing got a lot smoother. "She" saved us tens of thousands of dollars. Thanks Val!

My take on the psychology behind this transformation is that women trust women more than men in an anonymous relationship through e-mail. And men tend to be polite to women in this kind of online situation because they are thinking, "She might be cute." (That's just tacky, isn't it?)

The Pen Is ...

I don't like e-mail for communicating with my team. Don't get me wrong—I use e-mail every day. But when I have to communicate something complex, important, or of sufficient value that it really *matters* to me, e-mail usually won't do. Let me list the reasons why:

- It is impersonal.
- It is easy to miss, when it comes in with a hundred other messages in a day.
- It is hard to provide nuance in e-mail.
- Complex relationships or processes are hard to describe in e-mail.
- E-mail is easy to ignore.
- E-mail is discarded easily.

So what is the alternative these days? I use ... wait for it ... *a pen and paper*! Can you believe it? It is absolutely fantastic. This new discovery was so good in fact that I might have to go out and buy some stock in a portfolio of pen companies. I think this might catch on.

So what exactly is so great about pen and paper?

It is personal. When I put together ideas on paper, such as in a to-do list, a drawing, or a process diagram, it is clearly a personal communication from me (a human being) to the intended audience (another human being). This is often lost with digital communications, since they are abstracted away in the handoff between a device and another device.

It is hard to miss because it is a physical object. I have to walk over to my addressee and hand it to him or her. This usually is accompanied by eye contact, and maybe even an exchange of words. Oh my, how quaint!

It is relatively easy to convey nuance in a handwritten missive. The handoff of the paper from my hand to theirs allows me to couple the written record with some finger-pointing and explanation: "The process starts here and wiggles over here and then results in *this* ..." snapping my fingers for emphasis. Nuance abounds.

Complex processes and relationships are the perfect applications for a drawing with annotations, plus a verbal explanation. It does not get any better unless you are ready to produce a documentary for television. I am thinking of *Frontline* or *Nova*. I don't have that kind of time or budget, so my pen plus paper plus voice are going to be my choice.

A handwritten note and walk-by are hard to ignore. I am standing there. Go ahead then—try to ignore me. It won't work.

A handwritten diagram is apparently harder to discard than an e-mail. I have been writing these diagrams and handing them to my team for quite a while now, and the pattern is that people *keep them*. These diagrams get taped to walls, left out on desks where they can be referenced, and carried to meetings. They are real *artifacts* with a human intention behind them (almost gift-like, I suppose). That makes them hard to throw away. This is a good thing. Fantastic in fact.

- I can digitize these and keep them as permanent documentation on our company wiki.

- Save an archive version on your computer.

- Send them by e-mail anywhere in the world. The iPhone (or any other modern phone) has a good enough camera to digitize the thoughts.

- Also, our company printer does a quick scan to PDF format, if we need to.

In summary, if you want to communicate effectively, convey greater complexity, and have your information understood better and retained and referenced for a longer time, put the keyboard aside and pull out some white paper and a good-old pen.

Communication Frequency and Duration

Many companies and organizations have meeting-centric cultures and devote an inordinate amount of time to scheduled and structured meeting events. This can result in employee distraction, demotivation, and overcommunication. As a manager, one of the most important tasks on my to-do list is to match the level of communication to every person and to our task load. As in the tale of the Three Bears, there is too little, too much, and just right. I do my best to hit just the right mix of information sharing to keep my team optimally engaged and informed.

There are a number of variables at your disposal in managing the communication in your team. Among the most important of them is a decision about how you structure the regular and day-to-day communication with your employees. I focus on the following variables: duration and frequency.

- *Duration*: How long do you spend with employees when you communicate with them? How in-depth do you get when you meet?

- *Frequency*: How frequently do you communicate with each team member? (Once a minute? Once an hour? Once a day? Once a year?)

I will tailor these variables to each different employee. Employee experience, personality, and respective task complexity are all different, so my communication style is different for each. My personal style is to touch base daily with each employee for 30 seconds to 5 minutes, and then facilitate meetings between employees or the whole team as needed. I end up being a communications facilitator for each member of the team.

This is great for me as a manager, in that I get a daily personal update on all of the following:

- *Employee well-being*: Are they happy, engaged, and productive?

- *Task status*: Are we on track?

- *Facilitator tasks*: What do I need to do to move each project element along? Schedule specific meetings between individuals or the whole team? Remove obstacles? Get resources? Change the task specs?

This also allows me to be a boundary spanner, with intimate knowledge on business processes from product design, marketing, engineering, and sales.

The Curse of the Expert

Since you are dealing with your business and your particular specialty every day (and have probably done so for years), you are very, very close to it. You have a context that is rich and nuanced from which to understand it. This is great for doing well in your specialty and communicating about it with other experts.

However, this expertise and close-up perspective can be a serious problem if you are trying to communicate with customers or non-experts about what you do. Invariably, you *will* have to communicate with people that don't know as much about your specialty as you do—that is probably why they are hiring you or buying your product. When you do communicate with non-experts, make sure that you recognize the need to recontextualize your approach to make sense for them.

Establish Context

I often see experts give a loving and heartfelt explanation of their technology, and start off by launching right into the details: "What we've been doing is focusing on the chemical structure of the bonding agents is such that light and heat degradation is minimized, and maximum rigidity is exhibited within a mere three hours of curing time."

OK, so what are we talking about here? We have failed to establish a context to help your audience to get onto the same page with you before you get into the details. Set the context first. Then get specific. You cannot assume that people will be able to follow. Start shallow and work your way into deeper water once you have made sure that your audience is following you.

Here's an example of establishing context: "My partner James spent four years at MIT working on polymers, and we have started a company to commercialize them. We are working on aviation-quality glues for use in aircraft manufacturing." Then get into the details.

I cannot tell you how often failures to establish context come up at my company, even after months and years of correcting it. When we write marketing materials, the first drafts often assume context has already been established with the reader on one point or other. One of the most frequent problems that needs to be ironed out is the establishing of context before diving into details.

Put a Handle on It

I spend a fair amount of time listening to pitches from startups—software, Internet, science, and engineering companies mostly. Here is a common theme: "With ywidget.com you can combine multiple social media paradigms in one context, with platform-agnostic messaging when you're on the go, and a centralized interface that allows you to organize your lifestyle like never before."

Wow, I have no idea what this means.

I hear this type of pitch several times a month from startups that are really excited about how they are going to change people's lives through their new, innovative product. The problem with this is that I don't understand it. I know that there is some "messaging" going on, and something "social," but not much more. I cannot explain their business to myself, let alone explain it to others— which is what I would have to be able to do if I were to consider their impassioned communication to have been successful.

Lets imagine a scenario together: you are going on vacation to Europe for six weeks. In preparation for your trip, you have arranged all of your travel items on the floor of your bedroom. Take a moment to visualize what *you* would lay out the night before your flight as you get ready. Stuff arranged for your trip might include jeans, shirts, underwear, a toothbrush, toothpaste, socks, traveler's checks, a laptop computer, a charger cable, a cell phone, a charger for your phone, two books to read on the plane, a camera, a belt, dress shoes, running shoes, sandals, and more.

Imagining all of these items, what are you going to do in order take them with you? You are going to *put them all into something that has a handle on it*. A suitcase will work just fine, won't it? It has a handle on it for a reason: it is easy for you to pick up and to hand to the guy at the check-in counter at the airport. It is also easy for that guy to hand it to someone else, and so on and so forth. Your stuff can only go with you if you make it easy for you, your family, and various members of the travel industry to pick up, hold, and carry.

Your business messaging is like that assortment of valuable and important items the night before your trip. If you want your potential customers to be able to carry your idea and hand it off to others, it needs to have a handle on it.

Put a handle on it, even if that means that you leave out important parts of your story when you communicate to others. That is called *brand sacrifice*. It is better to convey the critical essence of your business and have it remembered by your audience than to throw the kitchen sink at them and have them duck and run for cover.

The preceding pitch could be rephrased as, "ywidget.com is all your social messaging, organized in one place." That is something that I could recall after a day or a week, and something that I could pass on to others with fidelity. These are the hallmarks of good communication.

Speech Markers

When talking on a detailed subject, I suggest adopting a habit wherein you provide your listeners frequent *context markers* as your discourse progresses. This helps them to accurately follow and interpret what you are saying—and that is, after all, the objective of communication. Here are some examples of markers:

- I am going to change the subject. Is that OK?

- I am making an assertion now; this is just a preliminary idea, so please feel free to challenge it.

- This is a question, not a request. I am not asking for you to do this, but am just asking if it would be reasonable.

- I want to make sure we are on the same page, so tell me if
  this is right. You said …

Using communication management mechanisms like these is in effect providing a parallel layer of information alongside the content of the conversation. By marking transitions in topic, confirming your understanding, and explicitly labeling the status of topic points, you reduce the chances of miscommunication. Context markers are an effective strategy for enhancing the flow and comprehension of information in any complex or technical conversation.

Strategic Thinking

Strategy is a charismatic word for *thinking ahead and acting in such a way as to optimize your outcomes over a long period of time*. I like optimizing outcomes and so do you. I spent over a decade as a martial arts instructor, and I can guarantee you that in that kind of environment, everybody wants to optimize outcomes. On the Judo mat, *strategy* means getting out of a bad situation in one piece. To support this desirable outcome, think about the following:[1]

- Know your options.

- Know your opponent's (your competition's) options.

- Know how the market and business environment can change.

- Have a sense of priority.

This makes a great deal of sense in martial arts. It also makes sense in business. In this chapter of the book I will talk about strategy—ways of thinking that can inform your decision-making and make your business life easier and more successful. These will help you to know your options and those of your competition, and achieve a sense of priority to determine which things should come first, which second, and which are not worth doing at all.

---

[1] This strategy was a core lesson at the Integrated Arts martial arts academy in Austin, Texas, at which I was the assistant instructor for many years.

A Human Flaw: Failure to Appreciate the True Complexity of the World

The world is a complex place. The human brain is highly adept at processing information, but depends heavily on abstraction and generalization to deal with the true complexity of the environment around us. Even seasoned veterans of any given specialty will find that unforeseen details will pop up and affect their plans. Account for what you don't know in your planning by adding in extra time and resources.

Even in a familiar environment, with a cohesive team, doing a project similar to projects that have been done before, there will be aspects that were unknown during the planning phase (Figure 6-1), and unanticipated in terms of allocating reserve resources for them.

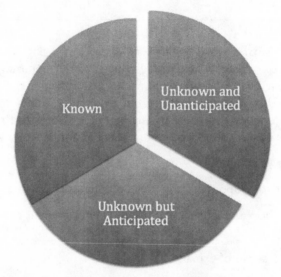

Figure 6-1. The three categories of events that exist in all projects and endeavors

In project management, you will see managers budget both time and money in anticipation of unforeseen problems. This is called *padding*. It never ceases to amaze me how much can be unknown in a project. I assert to you that the true complexity of the world in which we operate is *way* beyond our grasp. When we make plans and predictions for our projects and for our businesses, we make a mental abstraction of how the chaos and complexity of the world have bearing on what we are doing. This abstraction is a smoothing out of the wrinkles, a removal of the messiness, a simplification of the unknown mass of connections and relationships that actually exist into a clean mental representation of only the most significant facts. It is in guessing what is most significant that we can make our mistakes, as it is the nature of chaos that what is significant and not significant can change drastically and suddenly in a short period of time.

Takeaway: Realize that you will not be able to anticipate everything that will happen, and be prepared to allocate extra time and resources commensurate with the complexity. More complexity means that more will be unknown.

The 80/20 Rule

You very often get 80 percent of the result for about 20 percent of the work. For example, in the software world, a project that takes two weeks will often look done after just two days: the visible stuff will be there, and manager types will start getting excited about the deployment date being close (read: tomorrow). There is often a feeling that the developers are slacking off or even incompetent when it takes the rest of the week, and then *all* of the following week, to actually get the project code completed, tested, tweaked, retested, and deployed. As Figure 6-2 shows, the same phenomenon occurs in all walks of life, whether painting your house, landscaping your yard, or writing a book.

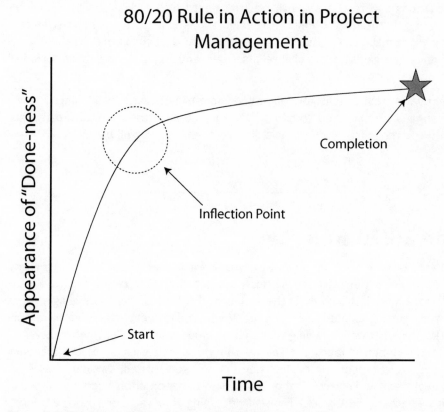

Figure 6-2. The illusion of being "close to done" can be a powerful one

Knowing to distinguish appearances from actual reality is a key skill in running a business. Learn to recognize the 80/20 rule when it is at work in your business and you will appear to be wise beyond your years. It is now time to grow a long, gray beard and stroke it pensively as you sagely predict to your employees that your project will take another two weeks.

Always Ask

Dr. Gaylen Paulsen, who taught an excellent class on negotiation at the University of Texas School of Engineering, gives one of the simplest and most effective pieces of advice I have ever heard:

> *Always ask for something you want, even if you don't think you can get it.*

He would challenge his classes to see who could get the most benefit in 30 days by using this technique. I ended up with about $22,000 of value in that month that I would not otherwise have gotten—just because I was willing to ask. Gaylen was impressed. (I am not sure, but even years later I may still hold the record for the challenge.) I got a corporate sponsorship to pay a large chunk of my engineering graduate-school expenses, a new car for $4,000 less than anybody would have believed, and several other small benefits in the weeks after being challenged with this simple idea. What did I do differently?

1. I decided to expect success.

2. I asked for what I wanted.

It works. Just adopting this mindset will be worth the time spent on this book 100 times over. I promise.

■ **Exercise**   *Always ask.* Try this yourself. For the next month, look for opportunities to ask for things that you want, but would not normally think you could get. Ask for an upgrade to first class at the ticket counter. Ask for a lower price, a better deal, or whatever. The point is to ask. The worst that can happen is that you'll be told no.

Ready, Fire, Aim

This method is aimed at a bootstrapped or small operation producing a less complex product with a lighter design cycle (consumer-facing web in particular). I prefer the ready-fire-aim method of management for most of my projects that fit in this category. As the name suggests, you will decide what target you are trying to build into using the best guess available at the time you start. You immediately start building something, and vigorously collect feedback along the way to create a suitable product. The comparison to artillery is informative: old-school battleships would come equipped with big guns on their decks. To hit a target, they would turn the turret toward the target, set the elevation, and select how many barrels of powder to put behind the projectile. As far as aiming goes, they would be *done* at this point. The gun would be fired and would either hit the target or miss. This can be problematic if the target is moving in unpredictable ways. The first shot will often be nothing more than a targeting aid, to be followed by a second or third shot that will be required to home in on the target. This wastes time and gunpowder, but it was the best that the Navy could do at the time.

More recently, guided munitions solve this dilemma. A projectile is fired in the general direction of the target. Feedback (usually a laser, GPS, or RADAR) allows constant adjustment of the path in flight. Even if the target moves, so long as the feedback loop is intact, you will arrive at the intended destination. Projects can be like this.

I like to build something small and quick, gain feedback, and repeat. This cycle continues until I have a product that works. I will almost never have a complete spec before getting started. Firing first and aiming later gets you to market fast, which is critical for small businesses—especially if your first guidance was close to the mark. This speedy approach also helps you to validate the market early. You can get out there and start learning, and get engaged in the market quickly and adjust (and even get out) quickly if need be.

Ready-fire-aim is particularly appropriate for consumer-facing web businesses, as there are lots of potential users and relatively low costs associated with development. The capacity to play this quick strategy decreases as the number of potential customers decreases. If you are aiming to sell software to enterprise clients (IBM, GE, etc.), then you had better have a very well-targeted product and a clear story of how it works and why it is valuable to the customer before you deploy or package your offering. Packaged and physical products and consumer goods are the same way—do your market validation and research *before* you build!

Tensions

Tension is the resulting pressure when two or more forces are applied to a system in opposition to one another. Business is, in many ways, the management of tensions. There are examples of this everywhere around us. In government, an example would be the classic American dilemma of small government vs. big government. In raising our children, we have the conundrum of helping a child to succeed vs. allowing them to use their own strength and learn from failure.

When addressing these problems, we should recognize that there is no right answer, but rather a balance of trade-offs. There may be one or more optimal answers that are as close to right as we could hope to get. These optimal answers are elusive. In a complex system (such as a business), the optimal choices for any particular subset of phenomena change with circumstances and depend highly on what your situation is, what your viewpoint is, and in what place and time you are at. I call this type of adjustable subset a *tension system*.

An example of this elusive optimization can be illustrated by President Franklin Delano Roosevelt's response to the Great Depression. In the long narrative of small vs. large government, he famously opened the government's bank account and began to direct public funds toward make-work building projects across the country. In retrospect, this is appalling to the small government camp, but it arguably did provide an answer to the dire economic malaise that was threatening the stability of our nation. Moving forward in time, as the economy stabilized and private sector jobs were created, it became less and less appropriate for that kind of spending and government intervention to continue. Taking the context of the 1980s or 1990s, the same set of actions would clearly have been inappropriate. In the 2009 market collapse, a similar spending pattern was seen again with President Barack Obama.

When addressing *tension systems*, the right answer can never be ensured. Instead of focusing on right or wrong, we position ourselves on the continuum of options, watch what happens, take feedback into account, and then either update or maintain our choices.

It is helpful to visualize tension systems as a continuum or line running through an imaginary space. You could visualize a temperature scale this way, with cold temperatures on the left, warm temperatures near the middle, and boiling hot temperatures on the far right. You can see that for a bath, the right choice would be warm, and for a margarita you would need to move left into the near-freezing region of the line.

This chapter will discuss some of the most common tension systems that entrepreneurs need to manage. The intended result is that you will:

- *Recognize them*: Many decision-makers are not explicitly aware of these tensions, and often simply ignore them or lock themselves into a position. Having an awareness of these systems will inform your capacity to recognize when data or situations are worthy of your notice. The ability to properly categorize data as you receive it is important when trying to improve your decision-making.

- *Plan for them*: Planning will also give you the opportunity to explicitly consider how each of these tension systems applies to your business, and to formulate a set of understandings about how to address them individually and in relation to each other.

- *Optimize them*: Your success in whatever you do will be, in part, the result of how you manage tension systems. Once you have recognized the trade-offs repre-sented by the continuum present in each of them, you will have the tools to begin explicitly calibrating your performance and manipulating your position in each. This active experimentation is the cornerstone to maximizing performance.

Notice that I have used the word *explicitly* several times. This is not a throwaway modifier to make the sentences seem more official or businesslike. I am using it to point out the contrast to non-explicit behavior (e.g., what happens by default, what we have seen other people do, what we have always done, etc.). By looking for, noticing, and then specifically responding to stimuli, we take a measure of control that would otherwise fall to chance.

Focus vs. Opportunity

Do you pursue new, unproven opportunities or do you keep a focus on what you think are your existing strengths? Don't let a relentless focus on "the plan" keep you from taking advantage of opportunities to make money. Doug Richard, a business mentor on the United Kingdom's *Lion's Den* television series, said, "My first business and many of my other businesses grew on the back of plan B or plan C or plan X." His was a business of adaptation and seizing on the best available chance to bring in revenue. (In Silicon Valley, this is called a *pivot*.)

This tension system is omnipresent in technology companies. Every project that I have ever been involved with has abundant opportunities to run this way or that in pursuit of "better" or "next." It is clear that one of the primary responsibilities of the entrepreneur or manager is to quickly (but gently) shoot down ideas that will distract from your purpose. I call it *skeet shooting*, and it is almost a joke between my team members and me. The tension comes in when you realize that some of these ideas are going to be real winners and deserve to be vigorously chased down and implemented. Telling the difference is a matter of experience, imagination, and paying attention.

Process vs. Agility

Nothing beats *just getting things done* when you are small and growing. Small companies are forced by circumstance to build product and rapidly make decisions as they grow. The process is often chaotic, but this agility (or ability to move, build, and adapt) is critical for them to get off the ground. As companies get bigger, however, a focus on just getting things done can cause problems.

A larger business has many more moving parts than a small one. Imagine if IBM allowed all of its employees and engineers to make decisions autonomously as to how product should be built, and to do so without consulting their peers. It would be bedlam. Chaos. At the same time, if IBM had too strong of a process mentality—with forms, documents, approvals, and meetings for every detail of its business—then it would not be able to every get anything done at all. IBM, as any other business (including yours), will need to find a balance. That balance will change as the company and the market changes.

You will find that there is a transition from the informal, non-process-oriented decision-making of a startup to more formal processes as your company grows in size.

Analysis vs. Quick Decision-Making

Another tension system you will find in business involves the trade-offs between analysis and quick decision-making. It is natural for many people to want to minimize risk by doing detailed analysis before making decisions. Others prefer to take a quick look at a situation, and start a plan in motion based on gut feeling. Again, these are both valid options, and either one may find a positive outcome across the various situations that you will find yourself dealing with in your business. The overall likelihood is that your optimal ROI will be found somewhere in the middle of this space.

I have been involved with organizations that I would accuse of analyzing too much—so much in fact that their performance suffers. I am sure you have heard the term *analysis paralysis*. It is easy to accuse folks of being in analysis paralysis when they pause to think carefully about a decision. The proof is always in the pudding, as they say, and there can certainly be valid reasons for doing a very careful analysis before leaping in and getting to work.

Certainly, the question of what is at stake will have great bearing on how much analysis should precede action in any given case. Sending astronauts to Mars, for example, should rightly be preceded by a great deal of analytical thought. As the analysis continues, the decision-makers will see that the inherent risks in the project will decrease as more knowledge is extracted or synthesized. At a certain point, however, it will be necessary to transition out of analysis and get into the "doing" phase of the project. The art here is in recognizing when additional effort begins to stop netting you additional benefit. This can be difficult because the effect of research on your outcome will not be known until later. You could spend an hour, a month, a year, or a decade putting together a stock analysis program for managing the 20-year return on your portfolio. You won't actually know how well it works in the real world until you stop testing and plug it into the markets with real cash and then watch what happens.

Knowing how much theorizing to do is an art form, and there is no single correct answer. We can recognize the extremes on this continuum as being foolish (e.g., ten hours planning a trip to the store or ten minutes planning a trip to the moon), but recognizing your real optimization point for your business situations (somewhere in between these extremes) will be a matter of experience, trial, and error (see Figure 6-3).

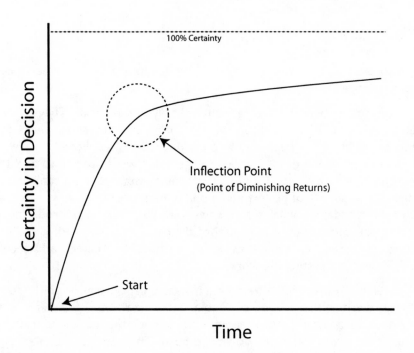

Figure 6-3. Certainty, too, is subject to the 80/20 rule, where it reaches a point of diminishing returns

One thing to take away from Figure 6-3 is that no amount of planning can completely eliminate risk. If you are doing something that is complex enough to warrant a thought-out plan, then there will continue to be risk no matter how you try to eliminate it. It is interesting to note that in business and investing, as risk increases, so often does the potential reward. That is one of the fundamental truths of an open market. This being the case, if you are planning for zero risk, you are probably playing for small profits as well.

Perfection vs. Progress

When is "good" good enough? Difficult question? When do you decide that what you are working on is good enough to call it done? This is a significant problem, in that getting it wrong can result in increased costs and delayed schedule on one side, and product failure on the other. One phrase that I heard long ago, and I must admit took me a little bit of time to warm up to, is this:

> *Perfection is the enemy of progress.*

To get to the heart of what this means, we can look at some experiences in my recent projects.

I have software engineers working for me that love their craft. They enjoy the art and science of what they do. This is usually fantastic, but it needs to be monitored. There have been times when a schedule has slipped and when a delivery date has been pushed back—things that I would prefer to avoid. On close inspection, one reason for at least a couple instances that I can recall was because of the pursuit of perfection among the engineers. When you are writing computer code, or building something with your hands, or producing anything that you care about, it is natural to dig deep into the art of it and strive to express yourself by making it as perfect as possible. There is a balance between this and just getting the work *done*.

The conversation that I often have with my team usually ends with the following: "Will rewriting that section of code and making the changes that you propose make the company more money?" Sometimes the answer is that it will keep us from having problems down the road. This can be quantified as the avoidance of future costs. On the other hand, the more frequent answer is a simple no. In those cases, I will ask for the code to be made good enough and to move on.

In almost all cases, doing a job as well as it can possibly be done will not make you more money. Again, the 80/20 rule comes into play (see Figure 6-4).

80/20 Rule in Product Quality

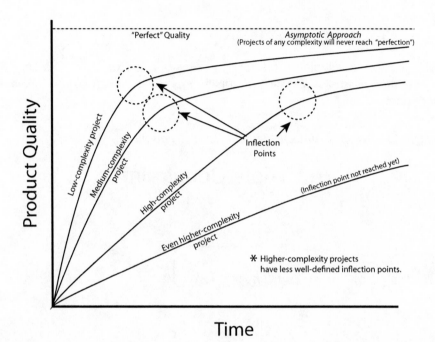

Figure 6-4. Quality will increase quickly up to about 80 percent, then reach a point of diminishing returns

The art here is again to recognize where the point of diminishing returns is, as it will not always be clear. A delicate consideration that comes with this cutoff of effort is that the more artistic or professional of your employees will be denied an element of satisfaction if they are not allowed to proceed further up the perfection path. It is a matter of incentives. As a business owner, you need to make money. A significant part of the benefit that a good employee will get from their work is a sense of accomplishment and self-expression. Needing to enforce this balance will hit directly at these two points, and the ramifications to employee morale need to be thought out in advance.

The Triple Constraint

When you are developing a product or executing a project, always keep in mind the *triple constraint* (Figure 6-5), which is explained simply by the following description:

Quality, features, and speed to market: You can pick any two.

The Triple Constraint

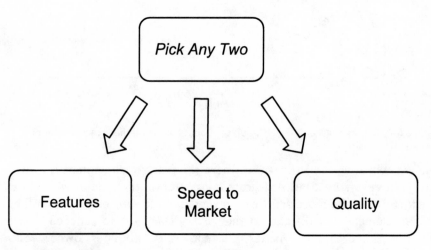

Figure 6-5. The *triple constraint* allows you to pick only two of the three primary product characteristics: features, speed to market, and quality

The classic triple constraint consists of cost, scope, and schedule. I personally prefer to look at speed, features, and quality.

Speed Plus Features

Our iWidget must be delivered to market by November 1 so that we can hit the Christmas shopping season. In order to compete in this tough market, we are going to pack the iWidget with ten new features.

The tight delivery date means less time to consider what the market wants and needs. There's little time to put concepts in front of the potential consumer. The planning portion of the project gets cut short in a race to get to the build stage. The development team races to get it all done, but it will take as long as it takes to deliver the features. Another fact associated with the timeline is that we *will* have to sacrifice some desired features, and we *will* ship the product with known bugs. It is unavoidable because the engineering team has a drop-dead date to meet. The test phase is likely to get cut short as well, because of the time constraints. The resulting product will be delivered quickly and have lots of features with lower quality in terms of targeting the consumer, and in terms of robustness, it is likely to break often.

Speed Plus Quality

We need the iWidget by Christmas. This means we deliver no later than November 1. I know that is a short timeline, and we need to de-liver a solid product so that we don't get chewed up with support is-sues, so I want to focus on one or two core features.

The delivery date means less planning time before getting started on development. The limited scope of features, however, allows the team to focus on what really needs to be done, so quality can remain high. The same holds true for development and testing. There are few variables to deal with, so a high-quality product can be delivered in a relatively short period of time. We are also likely going to have a cheaper cost of production on the product itself because the complexity of the design will be lower. The downside is that when the product reaches the market, it will be very reliable but may not resonate with a demanding public who is hungry for the latest-and-greatest features.

Quality Plus Features

> *We are going to build the best iWidget the world has ever seen. I want to have ten new features in the product and I want it to be rock-solid. I don't want to get any bad press about either system bugs or missing features. This is a lot to ask for, so we are going to plan carefully, build carefully, test carefully, and deliver when we are done. Not a minute before.*

We are focusing on building a great-quality product here. We are going to get out there in front of our customers and research what they want in a product. This means we are going to have a higher chance of getting the feature set right. We are also going to test the heck out of this thing to make sure that when a customer buys one, she is going to be satisfied with how it performs. We are running a risk, however, that we will spend a lot of money developing this because our team will be engaged with iWidget for a long time. This means the end product will likely have to be priced high, or we will have to sell a massive number of them at a smaller margin to make our profit.

The opportunity cost is such that we might have been able to build two or three iterations of simpler products in the same period of time that it will take to execute this plan. Also, the gap between our research and our product delivery will be long. This means we face to the possibility of being out of touch with the market on our delivery date. There could well be massive changes in the market while we are heads-down developing. Particularly important here is that our rivals could introduce new products that change user expectations, or there could be macroeconomic changes such as a downturn in the economy that could jeopardize our product positioning.

Quality Plus Speed Plus Features

> *The iWidget is the cornerstone of this company's survival. We are going to deliver ten new features by November 1, and we will have absolute quality control on this. Our company reputation is on the line with every product, and we are going to hit a home run with this one.*

This is actually the most common type of project initiation statement. "We need everything—and on a tight timeline." Especially in the United States, the business leader or CEO is supposed to be aggressive. "Always deliver more," he/she says. One result of this approach is that team morale can take a hit. When expectations are put forward that are not realistic, it saps the company's mental resources, making your company not such a great place to work. In addition, you nearly guarantee failure in some aspect of your project. The odds of delivering on all three variables are very slim. The leader that pushes for too many features and quality with an absolute drop-dead delivery date runs a good chance of a complete project failure. In case you need me to remind you, this is the worst of all outcomes in a project!

The takeaway here is that as a leader, you should modulate your expectations and declared objectives in such a way as to maximize the odds of success. In my opinion, "asking for everything" is actually nothing more than a lack of planning or vision on behalf of the decision-maker. Don't be that person. Instead, hone your talent for seeing into the process involved in delivering a project. Ask for more than your team will be comfortable with—that is to say, push your staff to perform—but understand the trade-offs that come with pushing too hard.

You may consider setting two separate goals: an unpublished realistic goal that is your best guess for your team's capacity, and a motivational "stretch" goal that will serve to rally your team toward higher performance.

The Positive Frame

Sometimes problems arise. It is a fact of life. It is a fact of business. Get used to it. And now I am going to tell you yet another thing that you already know:

> *The actual impact of problems is largely determined by how we choose to respond to them.*

When something happens that feels like it is going to derail your business or cause you difficulty, I recommend taking a moment and reframing it into what I call the *positive frame*. As an entrepreneur, you should carry this with you in your back pocket. There are two things to do to see things in the positive frame:

- Expect that things will actually be better with the change.

- Look at everything as an opportunity.

Some people suffer greatly when they choose a problem-based worldview. It seems natural and correct to them that everything that happens should be looked at from the perspective that it is problematic in some way. This is a very accurate-feeling model, because everywhere you look you *will* find problems if you expect to see them. (I suggest to you that we are such active participants in the creation of our worlds that if you expect opportunity, discrimination, or even Communist conspiracies as you go through your life, you will find evidence to support those biases as well.) The problem-based worldview is a common one in which the observer will often end up end up physically manifesting the actively created problematic reality with symptoms such as knotted muscles, indigestion, headaches, and a pinched expression on the face. Ouch. (Fair disclosure: I used to be that person.) The irony is that if you take the same situations and *choose* to view them as opportunities, you are also right!

For instance, some years ago I was advising an Internet software-as-a-service startup that was in the process of acquiring funding. The founders were upset as they complained about how a competitor had appeared in their space, where there had been none before. They were really feeling bad about their prospects and the loss of their hoped-for first-mover advantage. My advice to them was to view it as a positive development:

- Look guys, if there were no competitors, your investors would likely ask you what is wrong with the market. If it is a good idea, there will be other people going after it in most cases.

- Another benefit for you is that this competitor will help educate your future customers about the fact that software as a service even exists for this business. They are doing you a big favor in opening up people's minds in this way.

- They will also make mistakes that you can benefit from. It is much better to be a smart second-mover than an uninformed first-mover.

Choosing an opportunity-based worldview feels oh-so-much more fun, engaging, and productive than choosing a problem-based one. It allows you to stay creative, engaged, and effective when those around you need it the most; particularly when the brown stuff hits the fan—and it will.

Potential

As you read this, you are sitting somewhere, looking at this text (and enjoying it immensely, no doubt). As you lift your eyes from this paragraph, you can notice some of the details of the space around you. How much of that space could you see if you covered your eyes with your fingers? None of it, I would imagine. How about if you crack your fingers open a little bit so that you can see through slightly? How much could you see then? A big improvement over seeing nothing, but still very limited—probably a field of blackness with a single half-in-focus spot of light in the middle. There is a lot to see around you, but we can recognize that much of the space around you is invisible with your eyes covered in this way.

This is the kind of limited vision we often fall into without thinking about it. Beyond actual vision (photons hitting our retinas), other fields of information that are available to us get a similar treatment whereby they rest largely hidden from our understanding. When thinking about what possibilities the future could hold for you, and how you might take hold of some of those possibilities to change your life for the better, this kind of blindness can be very costly indeed.

Everyone in the world has this kind of blindness to some extent. Think about your own senses for a moment. Take a quick tally of all of the available stimuli that are coming at you, all the time. It would be unmanageable if we actually processed all of the information available to us at any given moment: sounds, kinesthetic sensations, light, smells, tastes. We only notice a narrow slice of these things at any given time. So we cope with this overload by having a narrow window of focus—like looking through a cardboard tube when viewing the Grand Canyon. We see only a slice of the rich and often overpowering streams of information that make up our environment.

In the midst of this real-time processing of stimuli, we will frequently pull back from the moment and reflect on the abstract field of *future possibility*. It is what could come; something not here now, but that could be arrived at with the proper actions. A problem with this exercise in imagination is that, as hard as it is to capture the true nuance of actual concrete occurrences around us, planning possible future outcomes is even less tangible and much less constrained. Recognizing this, it is fascinating to note that because it is less concrete, it is inherently much more rich and variable. *Unlimited* is a good word to describe it.

There is literally an unlimited potential for us as human beings to make bold, unexpected choices and experience fantastic outcomes—should we want to do so. But we are blind to it most of the time because that field of possibility is hidden behind things like tending to our jobs, brushing our teeth, and watching reruns of *Seinfeld*. It is an eternal truism that *you see what you see—and don't see what you don't see.*

I am going to make up a new phrase here: *potential field.* This is like the magnetic field reaching into space around a magnet, but it is a field of possibility as it extends forward in time and space from where you are right now. This abstraction of a potential field extends out from each of us. The many variations of this potential field represent all that *could* be. All that you *could* do. This potential field can be shaped and explored, but only in a very shallow and limited way, unless you are willing to break the repetitive patterns that hold you in the place where you are right now.

What would happen if you decided that you could question anything? What would happen if you could entertain any dream regardless of how outlandish it seems?

There is a potential of freedom moving in any direction from the here and now, out into the direction of your passion—a place where your fire is lit up, and you light up the people around you. Think about it.

This optimistic, anything-is-possible mindset is where the entrepreneur finds the power to do what the entrepreneur does. It is a big part of what makes an entrepreneur an entrepreneur. It is also, incidentally, often a learned skill. It is something that you can learn to do just by ... doing it.

- If there were no constraints on you, what would you want to do today?

- If there were no limitations in terms of money or time, what would you do in the next year?

- If there were no limitations in terms of opportunity, scale, reach, and impact, what would you want to accomplish in the next 20 years?

Think Big

You may be limiting yourself without realizing it. Do you believe you can be the biggest player in your market? If not, then why not? Your answer to this question probably has more psychological bias than actual provable fact behind it. There is, in fact, a way available to you to accomplish almost anything. Don't doubt it for a second.

As big as you are thinking now, look two orders of magnitude larger. Seem unreasonable? Do not artificially limit yourself and your success because of preconceptions about what is not possible. Look out there, think big, and allow yourself to see it all working out. See your success reaching up to the highest levels and it just might.

With this one mental change you immediately and instantly increase the depth, reach, and variations of the potential field that is reaching out into your future. This potential field is the mechanism that in its essence becomes *your story*.

Here is an exercise that illustrates just how far the upper bounds of this concept can reach: if I told you that you could do something completely arbitrary and audacious, such as write the name of your favorite pet on the surface of the moon, what would your reaction be?

I am telling you that it is so.

If you were inclined to do so, you, dear reader, could start in the next moment to formulate and execute a plan (that has a palpable chance of success) to put your mark on the moon as described. The plan? Take your finances, such as they are. What would happen if over the next 40 years you were as successful as Warren Buffet has been? There are certainly investment strategies that would earn you in excess of $1 billion over the next 40 years. For the purposes of this exercise, you need not believe that you can do it, just recognize that it is possible. Continuing the story, we also know that technology is rapidly developing. Commercial space flight is almost commonplace now, with governments and private companies both providing pathways for rich individuals to do things in space. It is not much further beyond the confluence of wealth (which we understand is completely possible) and technology (which we know is lowering barriers to space every year) that you find your purpose-laden trip to our celestial neighbor.

The purpose of this drill is to help you to exorcise your self-imposed limitations by sheer brute force. What I am looking for as you visualize this realistic scenario is the ah-hah epiphany when you feel, if just for a moment, a connection with this distant and challenging objective. The sensation is like water flowing out of a constrained and tight enclosure and reforming itself into a new and wider shape—reaching forward in time and space. I am willing to bet that prior to this moment you would have never considered that the range of possible futures included anything this distant and far-flung. Here is to flexing and exploring your potential field. Flex away!

The Flail

When people get into a high-pressure situation when the stakes are high, they often get flustered and think that they don't have any options. They will often get bombastic and try Hail Mary stunts that will almost certainly make any bad situation worse. I call this *the flail*, similar to when a child who gets frustrated enough will often just start crying and flailing their arms around. I also saw this frequently with adults when teaching Brazilian jiujitsu, which I did for 12 years. New and even intermediate students would get frustrated, and then go ape and forget everything they knew about strategy, what to do, and what not to do. This would result, as I said a moment ago, in a bad situation getting worse. Eventually, as they became more advanced, they would learn to keep their head on straight and focus on the basics when they got frustrated. That lesson was often hard-learned and only came about as the result of trusting their training.

At a recent industry conference, SXSW Interactive, I saw an example of the flail that was both embarrassing and unproductive. The frustrated CEO of a company was having a hard time connecting with his desired audience at the conference, so he hijacked part of a panel discussion by taking the microphone during Q&A and addressing the audience with a pitch for his business. I admired the guts it would have taken to do that, but the attendees thought this guy was disrespectful and out of line because he broke social rules. Not a good move.

Afterward, I had the opportunity to meet with the gentleman and give him very direct feedback on his stunt. The backstory for him was that he believed he had a fantastic idea and a real value-add for the world but could not get any attention. He was getting desperate and needed to try something.

The flail arises from the desire to get big results from little input, and a loss in faith in our ability to positively affect our environment through planning and execution. The problem is that the flail can undo significant amounts of work (as in damaging your reputation or exhausting limited funds). When the urge to flail arises, I recommend buttoning down and focusing on basics. Get back to the little things that each incrementally make your business go. Pick the most important thing that is not yet done and do it. Then progress to the next thing and the next. Keep it simple and focus on the basics.

The Bell Curve

It is true that nature behaves in both predictable ways and in chaotic ways. Among the chaos, there are both visible and invisible patterns. Patterns are sequences of events that express themselves in ways that can be predicted.

People and business are part of nature. Recognize that in business, as in nature, when you are looking at large sets of data (your target customers, your competitors, the individual transactions that contribute to your bottom line, etc.), they will have characteristics and behaviors that tend to fall into bell curve distribution patterns (see Figure 6-6). By this point in the book you have seen this pattern repeatedly—and for a reason. Nature expresses itself in this pattern across a wide array of circumstances. It is a metapattern of grand and wide scale, so by understanding this you gain insight into the behavior of systems as far-flung as consumer decision-making, project management, and water molecules evaporating out of a coffee cup. This is important stuff.

You can use this to your advantage if you have this image in mind when you project how your decisions will play out in the marketplace.

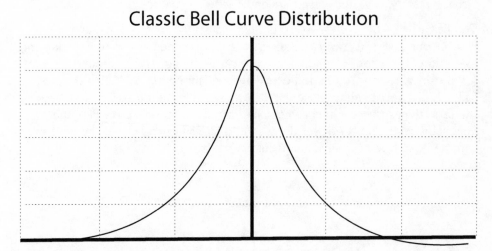

Figure 6-6. The bell curve is a global metapattern that manifests itself throughout business and nature.

To explain this, let's construct a *very* simple example. The archetypical make-something-and-sell-it business model of a pizza restaurant will help illustrate this. In designing a menu for our pizza restaurant, would you want to be *authentic* and write everything in Italian? It might be argued that people would probably understand enough. (Let's say the restaurant is in a historically Italian neighborhood.) It could more reasonably be argued that among the whole population of customers, a few would understand perfectly, most people would understand some of it, and some people would be completely lost. This is where a bell curve can be used to help you out (Figure 6-7).

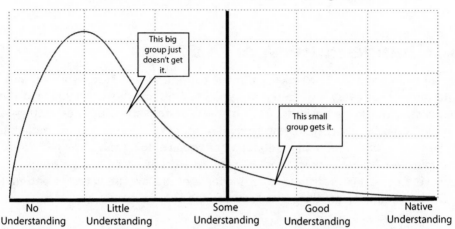

Figure 6-7. Customer bell curve for understanding Italian

Knowing that this likely distribution exists, you would reasonably predict that the "No Understanding" group is going to be totally lost, and at least half of the "Some Understanding" group will be lost. This would result in a quick decision against the avant-garde styling of a foreign language approach to your menus, and a decision to go with English as the predominant choice.

I find myself doing this kind of mental analysis for nearly everything that has to do with large groups of my customers. Deciding how to design a web interface? This leads to questions like these: what populations of people will be seeing the web site and what will their purpose be? Bell curve. Choosing words for marketing and advertising? Bell curve. Where will I be advertising and what mode of thought will people be in when they see my message? Bell curve.

For the restaurant, you might ask yourself whether you should buy the more expensive chrome barstools or go with the cheaper ones. To make this decision, you have to answer some questions. How many people will notice? Of that group, how many will actually be influenced enough by that small but expensive detail to be pushed them over the edge from one-time customer to repeat customer? Bell curves can help you tease out that answer.

A Change in Perspective

As an entrepreneur, you make it a point to look at and study your business and the market every day. Every day you feel you are the same you, and the business is the same business. Both of these statements are false—both you and your business are different from day to day and moment to moment. When you spend time thinking about what you are doing and what you should be doing, don't get stuck in a mental rut. Make it a habit to change your perspective on a regular basis. Here are a couple of my favorite ways for getting a new perspective on anything that I am thinking about.

Chunking Up

Expand your perspective. Look at your business from the 50,000-foot view and see how it looks. If you are absorbed in the day-to-day issues of running the business, you may not be in the habit of doing this.

If we were talking about chunking up with regard to a sailing ship, it would be taking your perspective up and away from sea level and looking at it from airplane level. How is it different from up here? For one thing, you see less of your ship and more of the environment that it is in. What if you moved up to a satellite-eye view from space? Even more so, you switch from object (the boat) to context (the environment and its patterns). Chunking up even more, you look at the effect of the moon on tides and how much light at night you have to sail by. Chunking up even more, you're looking at solar flares affecting your communications. Chunking up further, what can we imagine?

Mental exercises like this can yield new and interesting perspectives that you will never have if you confine yourself to your usual ground-level perspective.

Chunking Down

The geometric counterpoint to chunking up—chunking down—provides yet another set of real, relevant, and potentially useful insights.

To continue the sailboat analogy, chunking down would be looking at how barnacles clinging to your hull increase friction and drag, causing you to travel with slightly less velocity. Chunking down might have you analyzing the speed at which the crew can execute a tack to starboard or how positioning of the cargo in the hold affects your ability to handle high waves. The chunking-down methodology is critical for achieving operational excellence. From a business perspective, it is the process of deconstructing all of the details of how you touch your customers and optimizing all of the little pieces that matter—and judiciously leaving the pieces that don't matter undisturbed.

Systems Thinking

Let's take a moment to think about thinking. The Greeks taught us about *linear thinking*, in which logic and sequential analysis are used to come to conclusions about the world around us.

Here's an example of linear thinking: "Customers like coupons. If I put a coupon in the newspaper, I will get more business."

This is a valid logical structure—the kind of structure that we use hundreds (if not thousands) of times a day to make decisions. Having applied a label to this method of thinking, I would like to introduce you to an alternative way of using your brain, called *systems thinking*. Systems thinking is a way to think of many things at once (a system of interconnected processes) instead of one thing at a time (linear). Systems thinking will allow you to visualize your business in multiple dimensions, to feel the ebb and flow of the inputs and outputs, to feel the sense of timing and balance within it, and to effortlessly access the rich field of information and potentials that exist outside of the standard linear-thinking mindset.

Here's an example of systems thinking: "Customers like coupons. If we run a coupon in the paper ... I can feel a number of aspects of our business that change at once ... the ad spend ... branding effect of the reach of the ad (depending on the approach) ... distraction of marketing team from core business ... customer expectation of getting discounts may hurt us since we don't usually do coupons" (and 100 other things, all felt and wordless).

As an illustration of the process of visualizing your business from the inside—a systems-thinking approach—let us take a brief trip down the road together and think about driving. The next time you drive your car, notice how you are processing the experience. It will likely feel like the following common-sense statement: "I am sitting in my car and driving down the road." But there is more for you here ...

Try this the next time that you are driving: feel the steering wheel in your hands. There is vibration from the road coming up through the frame of the car to your seat. Can you feel it? Feel the texture of the road beneath the tires. It is interesting how the smoothness of the road is punctuated by minor variations in the concrete.

Allow your awareness to expand beyond your body and take in the whole length and width of the car. As you change lanes, accelerate, and decelerate, allow yourself to sense the car as you would your body. You can feel the whole car moving. As you drive, relax into the experience of the car as your body. This is very comfortable, and you are more in control and more aware of the driving environment than you were before.

As you travel, you are seeing that the road ahead begins to turn gently. You are allowing your awareness to expand forward ahead of the car and feel the curve in the road. When you finally get to the curve you are already pulling in unison with the change in direction.

There are cars and trucks on the road as well. You can feel them, too. Without words, you change lanes to avoid a slower truck ahead of you. Your awareness takes it in, and you automatically feel how its change in position and speed affect you.

Can you see where I am going with this? With this creative riff on a quick drive down the road, we are playing with something altogether different from a linear visualization of a body sitting in a car holding a steering wheel and pushing on the accelerator pedal. This is a transition from a separate, isolated, Newtonian model of a person plus a machine to a systems-thinking approach.

Systems thinking takes into account multiple simultaneous variables and inputs. The potential result of this is the synthesis of information and understandings that would be unavailable to you if you were thinking in a linear fashion.

As another illustration, I was recently on a walk in Zilker Park near my office in downtown Austin. Just 5 minutes from the office is a patch of woods that has within it a kid's summer camp facility. This facility has installed a 15-foot log, suspended by steel cables just inches off the ground, which is like a moveable, rounded balance beam. The first time I tried to get up and balance on it, I immediately fell off. Same for the second and third tries. I gave up that first day, and came back the next day. That time I got on the log again and fell off again. On reflecting on why it was so hard to balance, I realized that I was thinking about it all wrong! I decided to allow my systems-thinking mind to kick in, and let my thinking expand beyond my own body to encompass the log, the cables, and the ground. Suddenly (and without effort) I had access to feedback mechanisms and a way to feel my way into the problem of balance. I was immediately able to walk all the way down the log and back without falling off. The difference? Nothing except the way I was looking at it.

Thinking about this phenomenon, I took my kids to visit the park and did an experiment with them. My two sons (Mitchel, age 5, and Connor, age 10) were excited about this balance log and immediately tried to traverse it—and fell off. I let each of them try two or three times, and they teetered and repeatedly stepped back to the ground, frustrated. I wanted to try to get them into a systems mindset to see if they could increase their ability to perform this task.

I told them, "Let your feeling reach into the log beneath your feet. Feel into it and relax. Feel into the log and it will stop moving—you will be able to balance with no problem." I kept repeating this as Connor immediately stabilized his balance and walked the length without any problem. Mitchel then tried, and I repeated the same thought: "Let your feeling reach into the log beneath your feet. Feel into it and relax. Feel into the log and it will stop moving—you will be able to balance with no problem." The five-year-old was also able to walk the length of the log without falling. Both of them succeeded on their first systems thinking–assisted attempt. This is the power of a changed perspective.

I believe we are all wired *naturally* to do this. In fact, I think it is more basic and intuitive than language-based linear thinking. The trick is to recognize this fact and allow yourself to relax into the alternative whole system–thinking model.

In business, this kind of visualization is of critical importance to me. I make it a point to build a multifaceted model for each business that I am involved in, which takes into account a long list of variables. Examples are

- The product

- The customers

- The marketing plan

- The team of employees

- The geometry of relationships between marketing, customers, and products

- Financial models for marketing, products, and staffing

- Frequency of events such as updates, product releases, and so on

This list will be long enough to include every bit of information that you know about the company, the market, and the world at large. The end result of each of these elements coming together is a laboratory environment—a representation and model that can be used to test any potential change to business strategy, tactics, or operations.

The feeling of having the model in action is that of a morphable, multidimensional structure that can be rotated in space, twisted, analyzed, rolled forward and backward in time, split apart, and otherwise manipulated in any way that the imagination can create. For me, this structure is experienced from inside and throughout it. Key to this structure are the geometric relationships inherent in the business. How many customers are coming in? Are they online or are they real customers in stores? With what frequency? What percentage of the time do they actually make a purchase? What structures outside of the business are bringing them in? What is the timing and dependency model for the marketing plan? These questions are not asked in words, but by applying them physically to the model and observing how the feeling changes. The experience of it is effortless, and the field of available information is incomparably rich.

What does all this *thinking* do for you?

Having built the understanding of the business, and having assembled the model, the model is just waiting to be asked questions. But questions without words. What repeatedly has happened in my experience is that someone says, "OK, we are going to do *this* and *this* in the marketing plan." After plugging it into the model, there will be an immediate conclusion, for instance, that "the plan doesn't make sense, and here's why." What may follow from this is a 20-minute discussion of *why* it doesn't make sense. That discussion (with whiteboard diagrams to support it, of course) may take quite a while to work through because the logic needs to be translated out of a systems-thinking perspective (which is wordless and nonlinear) and put into a language-based linear model for sharing with other people. This takes time.

As I said, I believe that we are all naturally wired to do this. It is simply a matter or recognizing the potential of it, and turning off the language center of your thinking long enough to get inside and *feel* the relationships in your business instead of asking yourself in words. Take the time to play with this. I started doing this about 20 years ago, and I am still learning how powerful it is. I use it daily. It is where the "wow" factor comes from when bringing strategic guidance to my businesses. Let it be the wow factor for you too.

Know That You Don't Know

We know all kinds of things about our environment, our market, and our business. Realize up-front that there is a great volume of information that is hidden from your sight.

You don't know everything, even if it feels sometimes like you might be getting close. Wise businesspeople should be humbled by the complexity of the world and always stay in touch with the fact that much more is *not known* than is known. They also realize that there is no end or limit to how much they can learn—which means that what they know at any moment is always incomplete.

Domain Knowledge

You can analyze a situation or market and produce remarkably elegant understandings and mental structures to deal with it, it is true. But before making any important decisions, or even feeling confidence in your conclusions, make sure that you have adequately coupled this type of exercise with sufficient experience in the market itself. While mental analysis is a valuable and necessary tool, it is important to note that a *single missed fact* about any marketplace can invalidate substantial amounts of strategic planning.

Confidence is often misplaced by smart people who have had a great track record of decision-making in one domain when they jump the boundaries of that specialty and begin to ideate in another domain. The process *feels the same*, but lies on different ground with different assumptions and background facts. A fantastically smart energy industry executive, for example, has no business expressing confident, detailed opinions on the publishing industry (unless and until he jumps into that industry and earns his confidence by the process of getting to know the publishing business firsthand). Having success in one area using a rich palette of thought-tools such as those discussed in this book will absolutely make it easier to enter other areas of action, but your capacity to analyze is no substitute for firsthand experience and domain knowledge.

Enjoy the Drama

Just as I created the mailroom-to-the-boardroom scenario for myself, identify what kind of drama you want for yourself. For me, this meant that as a young man, I wanted to work my way up from basic entrepreneur labor, to being a business leader and to see first hand all of the steps in between. From a strategic-thinking standpoint, this becomes your overarching story frame from which you contextualize and understand how each chapter of your life fits together. This can be a powerful tool when it informs you what cadence and tone best suit your personal needs. This frame has within it many classical formulas, such as the comeback, the underdog, the tycoon, the philanthropist, and many others. It is how we use archetype to describe to ourselves and others what flavor of experience we represent.

Identify your ideal story, and then go out build it and enjoy the heck out of it. It may well be *what you are here for* at this time and place. Go out today and make it happen. There are no excuses for simply waiting day by day to arrive at the finish line. If you feel some kind of spark or a voice that tells you to get up and do something great, making it happen is less "a doing" or some great effort, and more a matter of getting out of the way and watching what happens. Don't delay. There is no time like the present. Enjoy every step, every failure, every success.

Exiting Your Business

This book is primarily about starting and running your business. A critical part of that subject is a discussion of what to expect when you make the decision to sell what you have built, and move on. It is important for entrepreneurs starting out to understand the big picture of what likely options and events lay ahead for them in this regard. In recent years (since the 1990s), the idea of selling out to investors or issuing an initial public offering (IPO) has become the focus of incredible amounts of media attention and the stuff of modern folklore. It seems that in tech circles, everybody knows someone somewhere who sold their business for millions of dollars, so it is natural to want to replicate their success in your own business. While it is my personal preference to focus attention on the process of operating the business, it is important to realize that for those businesses that survive and thrive, it is likely that at some point the idea of an exit will become important.

Selling a business is the culmination of a lot of work—usually years of it. In order to be acquired, you ultimately need to have something that others feel that they have to have. This means knowing the right people, being visible in the market, and being on the right side of an intense valuation done by investors.

I have had three exits in my career so far:

- *Private equity sale*: In the late 1990s my Meridian World Data business was acquired by private equity investors. The investors were not in the mapping-data business (until it bought Meridian), but thought that there was good potential in running Meridian as a portfolio investment.

- *Strategic merger*: That capital from selling Meridian World Data, and a few years of work, helped us develop a growing online retail business—but this operation felt underdeveloped in many ways. We approached and negotiated a merger with a larger competitor in Chicago. It had a weak technology profile, but it had great facilities and operational capacity. With our strong technology back end, and their much weaker operational capacity, the fit was too good for us to pass up. We merged and the gravitational center of the two companies moved to Chicago.

- *Acquisition by competitor*: Some time later, I joined a company with the explicit purpose of positioning the company for acquisition. From day one, the primary objective for me was to get the company sold. My mandate from the CEO to was change the engineering, marketing, product, and culture of the company to get the investors a return on the substantial investment they had already made in the company. It was an intense fast-forward rebuild of just about every part of the company in preparation for attracting the best possible buyout offer. With the successful industry networking of our CEO and a well-received reboot of the business, we had an acquisition deal 13 months after I came on board.

These acquisitions were not accidents; they were planned for, and they were the result of a great deal of deliberate work, positioning, and communication. As you start or run your business, here are some things to think about that will help you to position and prepare for an exit on the best possible terms.

Preparing from Day One

If you are running a business, you have numerous and daily opportunities to take shortcuts or allow problems to fester. These shortcuts can span a wide spectrum, including how you deal with taxes, legal issues, intellectual property, HR issues, bookkeeping and financials, problems with product quality, and so on. These types of problems will appear as issues for most companies at one time or another, and the way that you deal with them will have many consequences. Those consequences manifest themselves in both the short term and the long term. The short-term consequences of not dealing completely and properly with this category of issues are clear enough, and vary from problem to problem. The long-term consequences are such that they can easily endanger your ability to successfully reach a graceful and profitable exit from your business. I advise you to plan on positioning yourself for your exit from the very beginning—by keeping in mind that to exit and transfer your operation to somebody else, the complete details of any hidden problems will come out of the closet and be subject to the scrutiny of your potential acquiring company. This means avoiding shortcuts, and making a point to clear up the messy issues that sometimes seem like they can just be ignored. The hope that they will go away on their own accord is a false one—the messy issues just seem to linger, demanding your attention for their proper resolution.

In addition to dealing with tough issues in the proper way, your preparation for an acquisition maps very closely to the good execution of the operational principles discussed throughout this book. Primary among these are

- Having identified a clear niche in the market and subsequently taking ownership of it through effective positioning and communications.

- Having built your organization to be self-directing, or self-managing (staffed with employees that are trained and empowered to run the business without the principal owers).

Common Reasons for a Sale

Even if you want to operate, build your company to sell. Keep your options open. You never know what can happen to change your needs or outlook. Here are some events that can trigger an exit (planned or otherwise):

- A plan to build and sell from the very beginning
- A belief that the future of the niche or market is not good, and you need to get out while you can
- Health issues
- Relationship issues between founders
- Financial weakness (perhaps leading to a bargain-basement acquisition)
- An unsolicited offer that's too attractive to pass up
- Investor fatigue (you are not yet wildly successful, and your investors or principals decide they want to move on)

What Makes a Business Attractive for a Sale?

Simply wanting to sell is not nearly enough to get you bought. In my case, when challenged with the task of getting a business acquired, the thought process for positioning and building to accomplish that end iterates repeatedly over the question of what our strengths are, and what the market has and does not have.

What would make us attractive (or irresistible) in the market?

Here are some common answers to that question:

- A developed product that would be too much effort to duplicate

- Intellectual property that an acquirer could not obtain any other way

- Strong brand recognition

- Physical assets

- A significant customer base

- Industry-leading talent on your team

- A larger rival in your space looking for greater market share

- Weakness (an acquirer may believe that they can buy your company cheap for resale, or that they can fix and operate your company)

Relationships Count

Relationships with the right people at the right time account for a great deal of the opportunity that you will need to be successful in your business. The same goes for your exit. Your chances of finding a good exit are enhanced significantly if you have a robust network. So long as you have a good reputation and a good story to tell, the more people you know, and the more people who know you, the better.

An individual's personal network is usually a very slowly evolving structure—so get ahead of the curve and shore up your network before you need it. Make it a point to be involved in trade groups, investor forums, CEO meetings, and the like from early on in your business. Two of my transactions came about because of attending an industry event and rubbing elbows with fellow executives over a cold beer.

Choose the Front Man Well

Once you decide to sell, or once you are approached, consider carefully who the front man (or front woman) should be for your business. It may not be the smartest person on the team, the most experienced, or even one of the founders, but a good front man is a person that can open doors for you. Pick someone with the right look, the right words, the right swagger.

For the sale of our real estate dot-com project, we had this in our CEO. He was invaluable in that he looked the part and could play the role expected by the acquiring company. We would not have had a deal if it were not for the CEO's ability to win over the investors early on with "old-boy network" charm. It also didn't hurt that he was smart and had a lot of experience in transactions from his previous work. Our company was a good purchase for the acquirer, but this connection and networking was what made the sale possible.

A sale has to be a mix of the right numbers and the right emotions. The numbers have to add up to a good value for the acquirer. But numbers alone are not enough—you also have to set the right feeling and emotional tone with your potential suitors. Some say that emotion does not have a part in business, but I assert that it is frequently at the heart of transactions when businesses are sold. Part of that emotion on behalf of the acquirer is their feeling about the organizational risks involved in buying your company. This category of risk includes whether or not the people, processes, and hidden aspects of the business are really as good as you portray them. The organizational risks are framed and communicated by your front man—and this is a critical process. A good front man can open doors and help you to close deals that you would otherwise never have had.

Getting the Right People on Your Side

If you are looking to sell your business, you need to get your organization's financial IQ developed and working toward the right ends quickly. If your principal founders are not experienced with negotiating and structuring financial deals, you need to find somebody that is, and start working with them months ahead of any negotiations to sell or take on serious capital investment.

A lot of irrevocable decisions can happen very quickly in this kind of transition, and a lot of value can be won or lost in the small details. The investors that you will likely be dealing with in these scenarios are (probably) going to be savvy, sophisticated, and more experienced than you in terms of the business of buying equity and structuring deals. In the process of selling a business, it is typical for the entrepreneur to have significantly less experience. In my case, I have been in three major transactions over 18 years or so. That means I have had some very specific experiences and a reasonably diverse track record as an entrepreneur, but compared to a venture capitalist (VC) or private equity group that might do five or six transactions per year, three is not a very impressive number in terms of negotiations. I think about it this way: if I had played baseball three times in my life, I would have a lot to say compared to somebody who had never played the game before, but would be at a disadvantage against an professional competitor in the sport. Professional negotiators and VCs are (usually) good at what they do, and they benefit from the fact that a significant gap between their knowledge and yours can cost you a lot. Make sure your team has an experienced deal-maker engaged on your behalf. Jeff Olson, a publishing pro who helped me extensively in the production of this book, experienced this in his career when he sold part of his business to a larger competitor several years ago. The situation was typical in that he felt utterly and completely outgunned when dealing with the guys on the other side of the table during the negotiation. He wishes that he had had more support and experience representing his interests during that process, and will always have some lingering doubts about whether or not he got the best deal possible.

Knowing this, you should make sure that you have your own gunslingers at the table with you during any acquisition.

- Hire an attorney that specializes in venture capital and acquisitions.

- Bring in an experienced businessperson to help you negotiate. Look for people like this well before you need them, and build their context in your business over months and years—you will benefit in many ways from doing this, in addition to having them there to advise you in a buyout.

- Setting up a formal (or informal) board of directors for your business early on can be another way to have experienced businesspeople on your side to help guide you. Being a board member is a minor status symbol for businesspeople, and it need not cost you anything to get them to agree to serve as one.

Due Diligence

Any sale will include a period of investigation called *due diligence*, in which an acquirer will attempt to get inside your closet and look for any skeletons. Make sure you don't have any. Or, if you do, consider framing them constructively and proactively sharing them with your potential acquirer.

To get through due diligence

- Be free of lawsuits and legal entanglements. The uncertainty of pending lawsuits will scare away most potential acquirers.

- Ensure that you have maintained full and proper bookkeeping and financials.

- Provide all contracts and current legal obligations.

- Show that you have used intellectual property properly. In a recent acquisition, we went through two months of intense due diligence. Neither the principals on our side nor our attorneys had ever seen anything like it before—we were presented with a long list of disclosure requirements that dove deep into core software, servers, every agreement with every vendor, and even to the level of providing lists of every software program on every computer and laptop in the organization. It must have been good karma paying off for us, because we had meticulously licensed every relevant piece of software across our infrastructure.

- List reasonably well-documented operational assets (software, product production, and processes). Any acquiring company will send in its crew of experts and managers to interview your team with the purpose of making sure that they will be able to successfully utilize your assets according to their plan. This is where having documentation and well-designed systems can really pay off. If you are holding together your operation with layers of duct tape and bailing wire, you might not get the nod to go ahead during due diligence.

One fond memory of mine from when we were selling the Meridian company involved a comment from the investors. They said they "had never seen such a well-prepared due diligence package." Sterling had printed and bound all of the contracts and financials into a phone book–sized package that served as the centerpiece of due diligence. The full and well-documented disclosure set the tone for what was to become a relatively quick and easy sale.

Earn-Out Agreements

Investors like to hedge their bets. Many recent deals that I have seen, especially with smaller companies, have involved earn-out clauses in the acquisition contract. In this scenario, the buyer pays a percentage of the purchase price up front, but withholds the remaining money contingent upon you staying in the business for a couple of years post-deal and driving a prescribed level of performance. In essence, they are telling you this:

If you believe your own sales pitch about where your business is going, prove it by doing it.

They will pay you a percentage of your asking price to acquire your company, and hold out the remainder as "safety money." The remaining money will never be paid unless you can prove that your sales pitch was not simply hot air: You hit your multi-year business metrics and grow the company value to where you said it could go. This is usually 2 years in term. It is good to know ahead of time that your options on exit may involve this kind of time-intensive scenario.

Giving Up Your Baby

Every aspect of running a business can be imbued with emotional content for an entrepreneur. There had to be a serious case of fire in the belly for you to commit to building a business in the first place. It is a sure thing that there will be a significant emotional component in selling your company. In the case of Meridian World Data, our decision to sell was definitely an emotional one. My business partner told me, "If I have to do this one more day, I am going to shoot myself." If that is not an emotional decision, I don't know what is. So we sold it. Luckily, I was on the same page as my partner, and I agreed to do it. This is a significant point where controlling interest and management control can come into importance.

One very likely result of your emotional investment in a company (and your close-up perspective) is that you may tend to overvalue your business due to your proximity to it. Your potential acquirers will likely see things differently. They are going to lowball you—just try not to take it personally! In one case, we actually lost an early acquisition deal because we had momentary second thoughts about the sale price. We were near to a deal, and we were feeling the pain of impending separation from our baby (company). We mishandled the situation by pushing too hard for too much. That potential deal fell through at least in part because we had not worked out for ourselves what our pricing requirements were—and we let it get the better of us. We sold the company to another party within a few months, but at a lower price than had been offered in the deal we lost. Tough lesson. One useful way to keep this type of problem at bay is to decide early on how to answer this question, "How much is enough?"

Think about what an exit needs to look like for you to be satisfied. Set a minimum price that you would accept, and then anchor your negotiations well above that level. Also think in advance about other characteristics of the deal that will be important:

- Do you want to stay on and earn a salary as an employee?

- Do you want to get out and move on to other things? (Watch out for earn-out conditions in this case.)

- How will your employees be taken care of?

- Do you want your brand to survive, or is it OK for it to be subsumed by another company or taken apart?

Getting and Evaluating an Offer

The most primal of human emotions come into play when you finally get an offer to sell your business: fear, excitement, anger, uncertainty, greed, relief. It will trigger a significant emotional response. As Darwin would tell you if he were part of this conversation, emotions evolved in humans in support of our survival, which, when it comes to behavior, is often concerned with the acquisition and defense of resources. From a biological standpoint, selling your business is a major event. Short of being attacked by a bear or otherwise having your life threatened, few situations will be more personal or emotionally intense.

Here are some thoughts on evaluating an offer:

- Make an effort to distinguish between emotion and reason.

- Use tools outside of your own thought to help you to establish a depersonalized perspective—market data, advisor input, analysis spreadsheets.

- I always anchor my considerations on the big-picture scale, and then work my way down to the details. My process starts with finding an answer to the simple yet profound question, "How much is enough?"

Also, notice the explicit difference between "How much is enough?" and "How much can I get?" Economists will tell you that maximizing outcomes is the purpose of negotiation in the marketplace, but this is not just a money question. I suggest that you evaluate this question in a multidimensional fashion:

- *Finance*: How much money is enough?

- *Time*: Will this deal position me with enough time to do what I want in the next stage of my life?

- *Future opportunity*: Will this deal position me well for my next career step?

- *Stability*: Does this deal create aggregately more or less stability? Is stability even important to me?

- *Emotional satisfaction*: Does this feel like a fitting move in terms of how I want to write my own story?

Handling Employees During a Transition

If you are negotiating a buyout or merger, your employees will likely know something is going on, even if you are trying to keep it low profile. Transitions are scary, and what will happen is that in the absence of specific and consistent messaging from management, your employees will be forced to imagine some of the worst scenarios and begin preparing for them (getting fired or laid off is primary among these). While severance of employment for team members often goes along with acquisitions, it is the solemn responsibility of management to communicate truthfully and as openly as possible with the team as the process unfolds.

My objectives in this regard are as follows:

- Be as open as possible with information. Speak frequently and personally with individuals who want to know what is happening.

- Take care of employees in a fair and generous way.

- Allocate extra compensation for key team members if you need to ensure their stable participation through the transition.

Exit or Operate?

The idealized version of the fairytale startup sounds something like this: A couple of guys have an idea and build it in their mom's garage over four grueling months. They roll the product out, it catches the market's attention, and 18 months later, they have multi-million-dollar buyout offers rolling in. They take an offer, and live happily rich ever after.

An alternative, less media-worthy version follows. A couple of guys have an idea and build the first version of it in their mom's garage over four grueling months. They roll the product out, starting small, and they build up a loyal following of customers. They enjoy the business so much that it never even occurs to them that they would want to sell. They do take investments (in exchange for a minority stake in the business), which they use to professionalize their operation:

1. They move into new offices.

2. They carefully hire staff, including managers (that they know are smarter than they are), and begin sharing the burden of running the company with a team.

3. They position key staff members in roles that quickly get their business to self-managing status—freeing up the founders to focus on as much or as little of the operation as they desire.

4. They produce a steady income from the business that allows them to do whatever they want, inside or outside of their successful startup.

I think that the social commentary on the "big deal" may overemphasize selling out. Until the last several decades, the main purpose of building a business was to simply have a business, which meant building profitable relationships with customers, and building a team to do good, fulfilling work. As many find, the greatest joy is in the journey, not the destination.

Exit, and You Are Just Going to Want to Be In Again—Soon

Retirement, leisure, and the proverbial hammock on the beach are overrated, but they are great as a contrast to a period of accomplishment. They're the yin to the startup's yang. But all the time? No way (not for me anyway). For me, leisure only has meaning as an occasional contrast to building and working.

Notice all of the ex-startup folks that are now VCs and angel investors, interviewing and working with startups. One of the primary reasons for this is the thrill of the chase. The game is complex, primal, and exciting—carrying just the right mix of thinking, execution, luck, and potential financial upside to provide a powerful cocktail of emotional rewards for the participants. The lure of this game doesn't simply go away once you have made a some money by selling a startup. My read on this is that the ex-startup guys out there looking for ways to play are somehow less happy than the guys who are all-in and playing for everything.

There are few things that can make you feel quite as alive as being involved in a startup, feeling the high stakes and having a lot riding on how well you and your team match the current of the changing market. Live it. Enjoy it.[1]

---

[1] Find more resources on startups and business at the companion website for this book: http://startup-insider.net.

Index

T, U

CPSIA information can be obtained at www.ICGtesting.com
Printed in the USA
LVOW100453110412

277096LV00001B/83/P